First Book in Chemistry: For the Use of Schools and Families

Worthington Hooker

[illegible] [illegible]

[illegible]

15

FIRST BOOK

IN

CHEMISTRY.

FOR THE USE OF

SCHOOLS AND FAMILIES.

BY WORTHINGTON HOOKER, M.D.,

PROFESSOR OF THE THEORY AND PRACTICE OF MEDICINE IN YALE COLLEGE, AUTHOR OF "HUMAN PHYSIOLOGY," "CHILD'S BOOK OF NATURE," "NATURAL HISTORY," ETC.

Illustrated by Engravings.

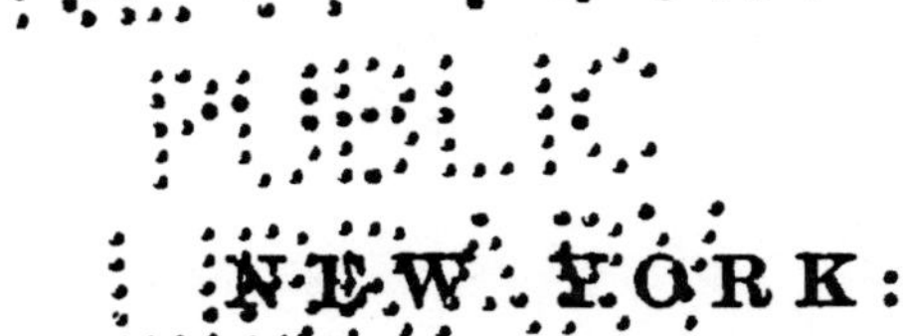

NEW YORK:

HARPER & BROTHERS, PUBLISHERS,

FRANKLIN SQUARE.

1862.

experiments, but illustrating the subject largely from common
day phenomena. At each visit I questioned them upon what
told them at the previous visit, and allowed them to ask me
tions. In this way I found out what they could understand,
what they wanted to know about chemistry. I was surprised to
how much of this science was within the reach of their capacity,
at the same time, could be made very interesting to them. Dur
all this time I jotted down my results, and at length put them i
the shape in which they now appear, so that the book was alm
literally made in the school-room. I may add that nearly the wh
has been subjected to the examination of one of the teachers who
rooms I visited, a lady to whom I am indebted for many valuab
suggestions.

This book can be readily comprehended by pupils of average ca
pacity of twelve or even eleven years of age, especially if they hav
gone through with my Child's Book of Nature, which it is intende
to follow. At the same time it is fitted for older scholars, to whon
the subject of chemistry is entirely new.

I need hardly say that there must be carefulness in experimenting
and that some of the experiments described in this book should b
tried only by teachers, or by pupils under their supervision.

This book is to be followed by three other books for the nex
higher grade of pupils. They are to be under one title, Science fo
the School and the Family. Part I., Natural Philosophy. Part II.
Chemistry. Part III., Mineralogy and Geology.

WORTHINGTON HOOKER.

CONTENTS.

THE

CHILD'S BOOK IN CHEMISTRY.

CHAPTER I.

THE CHEMIST.

IN this book you are to learn about Chemistry. But what is Chemistry? you will ask. This I will explain to you in part in this chapter; but you can not understand fully what it is till you become well acquainted with what this science can show you.

You see represented in the frontispiece a large room with a great many different kinds of vessels, and instruments, and apparatus. There are several persons, chemists, engaged in trying experiments. Their object is to find out of what things different substances are composed, and what effects will be produced when they are mixed together.

The chemists have discovered a vast many things which will surprise you. Each of the substances that you see all about you you are in the habit of thinking of as being one thing. The chalk with which you mark on the blackboard you think of as chalk, and that is all. But the chemist has discovered that chalk is made of three things put together. One of them is a gas as thin as air. In fact, it is a gas that forms a part of the air which you breathe. Another is carbon, or charcoal. Yes, the dark charcoal makes a part of the white chalk; but it is not dark now, because it is united with other things. The other thing in chalk is a metal. A gas, charcoal, and a metal, then, all three very unlike each other, make chalk.

Then there is water. Water, simple water, that surely, you will say, must be one thing. People used to think so—old philosophers as well as common people and children. But the chemists found out that it was not so. Water is composed of that same gas that is in the chalk, united with another gas with which they sometimes fill balloons. These two gases are uniting together to form water continually all around you. This is going on in every fire and every light that you see burning. In the flame that you see, whether it be flame of wood, or candle, or gas, or burning fluid, these two gases are busy uniting together to form water. You do not see the water, for as fast as it is formed it flies off into the air. It makes a part of the water in the air which is so finely divided up that you can not see it, as I have explained in Chapter XIX. of the Third Part of the Child's Book of Nature. But you can catch this water that is formed in the flame as it flies off, and make it to be seen. There are many ways in which you can do this. Here is one represented in Fig. 1. There are ice and salt in the bowl, the object of which is merely to make the bowl very cold. The bowl is held so far above the candle that the soot will not

Fig. 1.

gather upon it. Now the finely divided and heated water, as it flies up, strikes against the cold bowl, and is condensed upon it. A large drop of water therefore hangs, as you see, from the bottom of the bowl, fairly caught and brought to view. Considerable water can be caught in this way.

You can do the same thing with a silver spoon or a piece of tin, if it be cold. Held over a candle or lamp, dew will gather upon it. You do not catch as much water in this way as with the bowl of ice and salt, because the surface is not so cold, and is smaller.

You can not only catch the water that flies off from flame, but you can shut it up, as you see in Fig. 2. The candle here is placed under a glass jar, and the water first makes the glass dim, but soon gathers so much as to trickle down its sides. The air outside keeps the glass cool enough to make the experiment succeed. You can try this experiment with any glass jar, but you must remember to put some little bits of wood under the edge, as you see in the figure. If you do not, the candle will soon go out, for reasons that I will explain to you in another chapter, and there will be but little water formed.

Fig. 2.

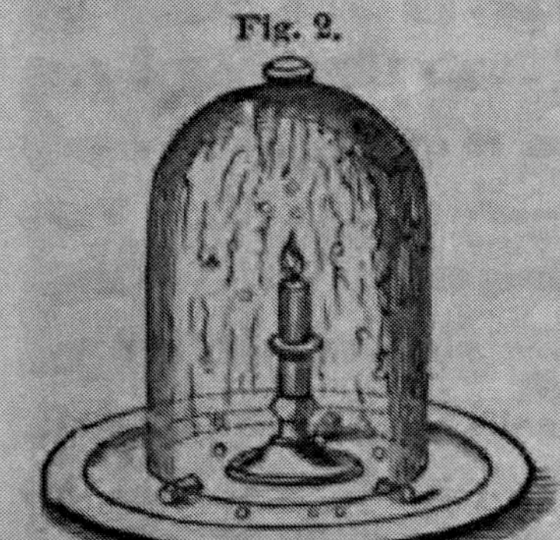

The water is *composed* of two gases. Now when the chemist takes some water and separates one of the gases in it from the other, we say that he *decomposes* the water. He does just the opposite of what is done in flame, for there the two gases, as I have told you, unite together to form water. So, when he separates the ingredients of chalk from each other, he decomposes the chalk.

I shall tell you, in other parts of this book, much more p larly about these and a great many other wonderful things.

I suppose that you have thought that you are too young know any thing about Chemistry, and that none but older wiser persons can understand about it. But this is not so. Th are a vast many things in Chemistry that you can understand well as the wisest man on earth. I shall try to select those thi only which you can understand and which you will be interest to know, and leave all the rest for you to learn hereafter, wh you get farther on in years and knowledge.

Chemistry will be interesting to you because it tells about many things that you see every day. I suppose that you ha been in the habit of thinking that the chemist is engaged in fi ing out only about things that have hard names, and that yo have nothing to do with. But it is far otherwise. Very many things that he can tell you about are the commonest of all things. I have already spoken of chalk and water. The little that I have told you about their composition interests you, and you will be much more interested when I come to tell you more particularly about them. Then there is the air that you breathe—you will like to know about that. The chemist can tell you what part of the air keeps you alive, and how it does it. You will be surprised to learn that some of the air is continually becoming a part of your body, your flesh and bones, and that some of your body is all the time turning into air and flying off all around you. But so it is, as I shall by-and-by show you.

Chemistry will tell you how fires and lights burn. You will find that there is a great deal of chemistry in so common a thing as a candle. There is enough to talk about for hours. The most distinguished chemist in England lately delivered six lectures to a young audience in London on the "Chemical History of a Candle," and they have been published, making a book of over 200 pages.

Chemistry will tell you what it is that makes bread rise, and how it is that the grain from which it is made is fitted in growing to nourish your body.

It will tell you how wine is made from grapes and other fruits; and explain what that is in the making of cider and beer which is called *working*. It will explain, too, the making of vinegar.

It will tell you how soaps are made, and explain the way in which they operate in cleansing clothes and other things from dirt.

It will tell you about the making of different paints and dyes.

About these and very many other common things Chemistry can tell you a great deal that will interest you, and will be of use to you as you grow up to be men and women. And you can know much about these and other subjects, young as you are, that the wisest chemists did not know fifty years ago, for chemists have discovered many facts that were not known then.

You hear a great deal about the experiments that the chemists try. In this book I shall tell you of many experiments that you can try for yourselves. You can try them with bottles and tubes that you can buy with a very little money, and many of them you can try even with what you can pick up about house at your own home by exercising a little contrivance.

But you will not need to do even this to be interested in Chemistry, because there are things happening before you continually that illustrate the subject. There are experiments, as we may say, going on all around you and even within you; and you have only to look and to think, to get Chemistry out of the commonest things. Every time that you rub a match, or set fire to gas, or a candle, or wood, or strike fire with your heel, you try a chemical experiment. Every time that you draw a breath, you make chemical work for your lungs. Every time that you eat, you set a going in your stomach some of the chemical operations that the chemist in his laboratory sets a going in some of his queerly-shaped glass vessels. And your body is kept warm, as I shall show you in one of the chapters of this book, by a sort of chemical fire in you—a fire without a flame.

Questions.—What do chemists do? Of how many things is chalk composed? What are they? Which of them are solid substances? Why is not the charcoal dark in the chalk? What did all people use to think about water? What have the chemists found out about it? Tell about the formation of water in flame. Why do you not see the water that is formed? How can you catch the water as it flies off? Tell about catching it with a spoon. Tell about catching it from a candle under a jar. What is decomposition? Why can you expect to understand much about chemistry in studying this book? Why will chemistry be interesting to you? What are some of the things that chemistry will show you about air? What is said about the chemistry of a candle? What can the chemist tell you about bread? What other things will Chemistry explain to you? What is said about experiments?

CHAPTER II.

OXYGEN.

Oxygen. That is a hard word, you will say. Why hard? Simply because it is new, and you do not understand what it means. When I have told you what oxygen is, and related to you the interesting facts about it, the word will be as easy to you as any other word of the same length of which you know the meaning. The names of many of your acquaintances would be hard words to you if they were not the names of those that you know. Now I expect to make you as well acquainted with oxygen as you are with any of your friends, and then it will be quite as easy a name to you as Joseph, or Caroline, or Elizabeth. There are many words which you use every day that are much longer than oxygen, such as amusement, dissatisfaction, experiment, etc.; but they are easy to you, because you know what they mean, and you are familiar with them. And so, when you have gone through this book, oxygen and other terms now new to you, and therefore hard, will be easy to you, because you have become familiar with their meaning and use.

Although you are not yet acquainted with oxygen, you have a great deal to do with it. Indeed, you could not have done without it at any moment since you were born. Every time that you take a breath you take some of it into your lungs, for there is plenty of it in the air. If what there is of it in the air should be taken out of it, you would die as quickly as you would if you were under water.

This oxygen is part of the food, the nourishment of your body. It does not, it is true, go into your stomach, but still it is just as necessary food for your body as the food that you swallow. It is food that goes into the lungs, and the lungs must have it, or you will die.

The food that you put into your stomach you can do without for some time. You can live without it even for days; but the lung-food you must have every minute.

The food that goes into you by your lungs helps to make up the solid part of your bodies—your bones, muscles, skin, etc. But it is not solid when it goes in. It is a gas. There are a great many different kinds of gases or airs. The air that you breathe is a mixture of these gases. The gas that we burn is a very different gas from that we have in the air. If you live in a village, perhaps you never saw gas burning from a gas-burner. But you see gas burning every day when you see a flame of any kind, whether it comes from wood, or coal, or a candle, or a lamp. The oil or tallow is changed into gas before it burns. What we call flame is burning gas. When wood or coal is burned, all except the ashes that are left goes off into the air, and burns as it goes.

Most gases have no color, and you can look through them as you look through glass. You are always looking through gases, for the air, as I have told you, is a mixture of three gases. You can not see the air, and so you can not see any gas that has no color. For example, if a gas-burner be left open without being lighted, you can not see the gas coming out, although you can smell it. The colorless gases are said then to be perfectly *transparent*, like clear glass, because objects are seen or *appear through* them, *trans* being the Latin for through.

I shall tell you about many different gases in this book, but now I must speak particularly of oxygen.

Oxygen, besides being a part of the air, is a part of almost every thing that you see. It forms a large part of all the water in the world. As I have already told you, it is in your skin, and muscles, and bones, and every part of your bodies, and is the most important part of the blood that runs in your veins and arteries. It is in all animals and all plants. It makes a part of the ground beneath your feet, and even the solid rocks are made in part of oxygen. This gas is the most abundant substance in the world, and so it is more in use than any other substance.

It may seem strange to you that so light and thin a substance as gas is can make a part of any solid, as flesh or bone. But you see every winter a liquid become solid, for ice is solid water. Now this same water, that is sometimes liquid and sometimes solid, is sometimes also as thin as air or gas. There is always some water in the air, even when it seems to be very dry; and as in the clear air that seems so dry there is no water to be seen, the water must be as thin as the air itself. It is no more strange that oxygen gas can become a part of a solid, than that this water, as thin as gas, can be turned into solid ice.

Oxygen gas can be separated from some of the substances with which it is united, and so can be obtained alone by itself. The chemist commonly uses for this purpose a certain powder. What this powder is I will not tell you now, but shall notice its compo-

Burning various substances in oxygen.

There are many beautiful experiments that can be tried with oxygen. I will notice some of them.

Put a lighted candle into a jar of oxygen, as in Fig. 5. It will burn now with a dazzling brightness, and will be rapidly consumed. The reason is this. It is the oxygen in the air that makes the candle burn at all. Of course, the more oxygen gets to the candle, the brighter will it burn. Now only about one fifth of the air is oxygen, and so the candle will burn five times as fast and as brightly as in common air.

Fig. 5.

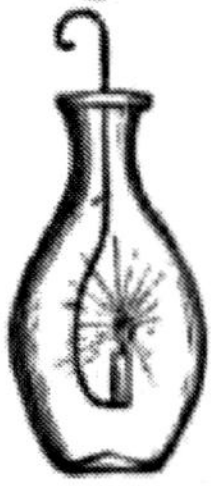

Fig. 6.

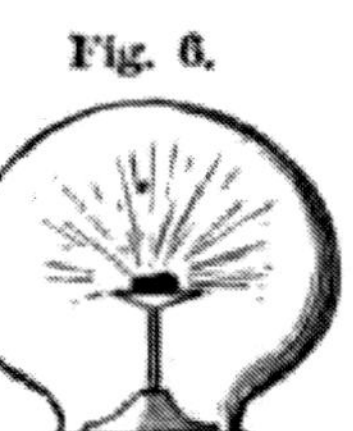

For the same reason, if a lighted piece of charcoal, which, you know, in the air is only of a dull red color for a little while, and then goes out, be placed in a jar of oxygen, it will burn very actively, and throw off sparks all around, as represented in Fig. 6.

Fig. 7.

There is no substance that makes so brilliant a light on burning in oxygen as phosphorus, Figure 7. A very thick white smoke arises, which is most brilliantly illuminated.

Fig. 8.

If sulphur be burned in oxygen gas, the smoke has a most beautiful blue color; and the smoke is arranged in a very singular way, as seen in Fig. 8.

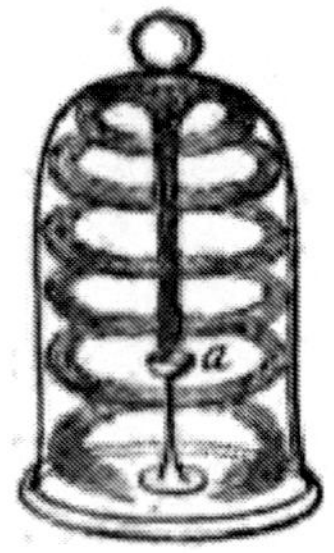

mon household things available. Professor Porter has very prettily shown this in his Chemistry—a phial, a test tube, a bowl, some tobacco-pipes, and a spirit lamp being all that is necessary in some cases. Glass tubes are often very convenient. These can be bent readily into any required shape by heating over a spirit lamp. Holes can be made through corks with a round file, so that the tubes can be passed through them.

it goes up straight in the middle of the jar, and then falls in curious rings down the sides.

There are some substances which most people think can not burn at all, that will burn very readily in oxygen. Iron is one of these. If you take a piece of steel wire, and twist it as you see in Fig. 9, you can make a splendid fire with it in the oxygen. But how will you manage it? You can not set it on fire in the air, and then introduce it into the oxygen, as is done with the phosphorus, charcoal, etc. It is managed in this way. The end of it is dipped in sulphur, or has a bit of something which will burn in common air fastened to it, as cotton or charcoal. You light this substance, and then introduce the wire into the jar of oxygen. The substance on the end of the wire, in burning, sets fire to the wire itself, and now the sparks fly most merrily.

Fig. 9.

Questions.—What is said about the word oxygen? How do you have a great deal to do with oxygen? What would happen to you if you could not get oxygen into your lungs? What is said about oxygen as food? Give the comparison between stomach-food and lung-food. What does oxygen gas help to make in your body? What is flame? Of what is the gas made in a candle or lamp? What is said about gases being transparent? What does the word transparent come from? Mention some of the things in which there is oxygen. What is said about its making a part of solid substances? Tell about obtaining oxygen gas. Describe the pneumatic trough, and the way in which it is used in collecting gas in jars. Describe the apparatus represented in Fig. 5. Describe and explain the experiment with a lighted candle. Give the experiment with charcoal. How does phosphorus burn in oxygen? Describe the experiment with sulphur. Describe the experiment with iron.

CHAPTER III.

NITROGEN.

To every gallon of oxygen in the air there are about four gallons of another gas called nitrogen.

This gas is very different, in some respects, from oxygen. Nothing will burn in it. Suppose that you have two jars, in one of which is oxygen, and in the other nitrogen. If you put a lighted candle into the jar of oxygen, it will, you know, burn brighter than it does in the air. But if you take it out of the oxygen, and put it into the jar of nitrogen, it will go out. Not even phosphorus will burn in nitrogen. So, if all the oxygen should be taken out of the air, every fire and light would go out.

Besides this, no animal can live in nitrogen gas. If you put a mouse into a jar of oxygen he will be more lively than in common air, and will act as if he were crazy, jumping about in the most singular manner; but if you should put him into a jar of nitrogen, he would die at once. And if all the oxygen should be taken out of the air, all animals would die, just as all the fires and lights would be extinguished.

But this nitrogen gas does not really put out fires and lights. A light, when placed in a jar of nitrogen, goes out merely because there is no oxygen. It must have oxygen to keep on burning. Only put a little oxygen in with the nitrogen, and the candle will burn; for it does burn well in a mixture of oxygen and nitrogen, that is, common air, in which there is four times as much nitrogen as oxygen.

So, too, nitrogen does not kill any animal, although he can not live in it. It does not act as a poison when it goes into the lungs; for there is going into the lungs of all animals, all the time, four times as much nitrogen as oxygen. The mouse dies in the jar of nitrogen simply because nitrogen can not keep him alive, as oxygen does.

Of what use, then, is the nitrogen in the air, as it does not help to make any thing burn, or keep any thing alive? I will tell you.

Suppose that the air were all oxygen instead of being a mixture of oxygen and nitrogen. What would happen? You can see by calling to mind the experiments in which different things were burned in jars of oxygen. Our fires and lights would burn very brightly. This would sometimes be quite convenient. We should not be troubled with dull fires and dim lights. It would be one of the easiest things in the world to kindle up a fire. But then, on the other hand, there would be a great deal of inconvenience and danger from so much oxygen. Things would burn too fast. They would be too ready to take fire. We should have things taking fire much oftener than now; and when a fire once was a going, it would be very hard to put it out. If a block of houses should take fire at one end, there would be no stopping the fire; it would go through the whole block. Whole towns and cities would be often burned up. The sparks from locomotives would be continually setting fire to some bridge, or fence, or house. We should have to be much more careful about fire than

we now are, and it would be one of the chief occupations of . put out fires.

Besides all this, if the air were wholly oxygen it would b jurious to all animals. It would be too heating, too stimula With so much oxygen going into our lungs, we should be all time as hot as we are after exercising violently. This wo make us very uncomfortable. We should be forever fanni ourselves, and drinking cold water, and seeking for cold air. I flammations and fevers would be produced, and we could not li long in this way.

It is chiefly for these reasons that God has given us our oxy gen mingled with so much nitrogen. It is very much as we take some medicines. They are put into sugared water because it would not do for us to take them clear. The sugared water is to the medicine as the nitrogen is to the oxygen. Suppose the medicine is some strong acid. It would make your mouth sore if you should take it clear, so we *dilute* it, as we say, with sugared water. In like manner, the oxygen is diluted with nitrogen, that we may take it into the lungs without harm.

Nitrogen, you see, is a very mild sort of thing. It just goes along every where with the smart and lively oxygen, and keeps it from doing too much in the ways that I have mentioned. But you will find, before you get through with this book, that nitrogen is, after all, no milk-and-water character. It is ready to do when there is need of its doing, and it unites with many substances to do some very smart things. I will mention here only two examples of this. Nitrogen unites with oxygen, as you will see in the next chapter, to form one of the most powerful acids in the world, aqua fortis. It is also one of the two ingredients of ammonia, or hartshorn, which so tingles your nose whenever you smell it.

You can get nitrogen gas from the air by a very pretty experiment. All that you need is a large basin, a good-sized glass jar, a flat cork smaller than the open end of the jar, some powdered chalk, and a bit of phosphorus. Fill the basin with water; hollow out a little place on the cork and sprinkle some chalk into it; place the phosphorus on the chalk, and then put the cork into the water. Setting fire to the phosphorus, you put the jar over it with its edge in the water. Think, now, what you have in the jar. There is a mixture of oxygen and nitrogen, that is, air. Then you have the burning phosphorus. Now the phosphorus burns because there is oxygen there. If there were nothing but nitrogen in the jar it would not burn at all. If you watch the experiment you will soon see that the phosphorus burns rather dimly, and at length goes out, although there may be considerable phosphorus left on the chalk. Why is this? It is because the oxygen is all gone, and there is nothing now but nitrogen in the jar.

You will see that the cork has risen in the jar, being pressed up by the water. Why? The part of the air in the jar which is oxygen is used up, and so makes room in the jar, and the water and cork are pressed up to fill this room. One fifth of the air in the jar is gone, for oxygen makes one fifth of the air. There is, then, this amount of room made in the jar.

But what has become of the oxygen? It is not lost in the burning. It is united with the phosphorus, and they, together, form the white smoke which arises when phosphorus is burned.

in oxygen, as represented in Fig. 7. This smoke is as ... the oxygen and the phosphorus make together, called ph... acid. This soon disappears, and the reason is that the ... the water so much that it just goes down and unites with ... leaves the nitrogen alone in the jar.

In this experiment the nitrogen is let alone. The burning ... phorus will have nothing to do with it, but takes all the ... out of its company. The phosphorus likes the oxygen ... ready to join company with it; or, as the chemists say, it ... affinity for oxygen, while it has not for nitrogen.

You will want to know how much phosphorus to use. ... jar will hold a quart, a piece of phosphorus twice the size ... large pea will be needed. As phosphorus takes fire easily, ... caution is required in managing it.

Questions.—What proportion of air is nitrogen? Tell about putting a ... candle in this gas. What would happen to the fires and lights if all the ... were taken out of the air? Tell about the difference between oxygen and nit... in regard to life. Why does a light go out when put into nitrogen gas? Why ... an animal die when put into it? Tell what would happen to fires and lights ... air were all oxygen. What influence would it have on animals? Of what ... the nitrogen in the air? Give the comparison of the medicine in sugared ... What does the word *dilute* mean? What is said about the character of nitro... What two very active substances are partly composed of it? Tell how you w... arrange your apparatus for obtaining nitrogen. What now is the jar filled w... Why does the phosphorus burn? Why does the cork rise in the jar? What ... comes of the oxygen in the jar? How is it that the nitrogen is left alone in the jar

CHAPTER IV.

AQUA FORTIS AND THE LAUGHING GAS.

IN air, as you have seen, oxygen and nitrogen are only mixed [illegible]gether. The oxygen is diffused through the nitrogen as alco[illegible]ol is diffused through water when they are mixed. But oxy[illegible]en and nitrogen can be united together in such a way as to form [illegible]ompounds* that are very different from the mixture that we call air.

One of these compounds is nitric acid. This is called [illegible] [illegible]ortis, which is the Latin for strong water, because it is so [illegible] powerful an acid. It will eat cloth, and even flesh, if dropped [illegible]pon it. How strange it is that such a biting acid is composed of two gases that are so quietly going into our lungs every time that we breathe!

These gases, mixed together so thoroughly in the air, [illegible] disposition to unite together to form this acid. It is very difficult to make them unite. All the shaking which the air gets in vi[illegible]olent winds and whirlwinds will not do it. Air is sometimes [illegible] heated, but the heat of the hottest furnace can not unite the oxygen and the nitrogen of the air in the furnace together. [illegible] of lightning, as it passes along through the air, will make [illegible] unite so as to form nitric acid; but there is only a little of [illegible] in this way. This little, however, being carried down in [illegible] is of use to the farmer and the gardener in making things

[illegible]

Now a person in breathing this gas [illegible] oxygen and nitrogen as he does when breathing [illegible] not merely mixed as they are in air [illegible] make a new thing different from both [illegible] as they do when they unite to form nitric acid. [illegible] of oxygen, or their mixture in air, ever produces [illegible] delirium, as does their compound, the laughing gas.

Observe how these two compounds, nitric acid and the laughing gas, differ from each other. One is a liquid which [illegible] corrodes. The other is a gas, soft and mild, but when [illegible] it makes people crazy. It is so generally disposed to make [illegible] pleasant and laughing that this has given it its name.

The reason of the difference between the two is in the different proportions of the ingredients. The nitric acid has a great [illegible]

grow. How this is you will learn, when you are a little older, in the next book that I will give you on Chemistry.

There is another compound of these two gases which is of a very different character from the nitric acid. It is in the form of a gas. It can be breathed, and it does not irritate the lungs. It produces, however, a very singular effect upon the system, making the person who breathes it delirious. In this delirium persons act very differently from each other. One, perhaps, bows and smiles continually; another dances; another tries to kiss all the ladies present; another laughs; another declaims with great eloquence; another wants to fight—and so on. The delirium lasts, at farthest, but a minute or two commonly; and when the person comes to himself he does so all at once, and seems to be half ashamed of what he has been doing.

Now a person in breathing this gas takes into his lungs oxygen and nitrogen as he does when breathing air; but they are not merely mixed, as they are in air, but are a compound. They make a new thing, different from both the oxygen and nitrogen, as they do when they unite to form nitric acid. Neither nitrogen or oxygen, or their mixture in air, ever produces an intoxicating delirium, as does their compound, the laughing gas.

Observe how these two compounds, nitric acid and the laughing gas, differ from each other. One is a liquid which stains and corrodes. The other is a gas, soft and mild, but when breathed it makes people crazy. It is so generally disposed to make them pleasant and laughing that this has given it its name.

The reason of the difference between the two is in the different proportions of the ingredients. The nitric acid has a great deal more of oxygen in it than the laughing gas has. It has just five times as much; that is, to every pound of nitrogen there is five times as much oxygen in nitric acid as there is in the laughing gas.

There are three other compounds of oxygen and nitrogen, making five in all. The proportions of oxygen in them are exactly as 1, 2, 3, 4, and 5. The laughing gas has the smallest proportion, 1, and the nitric acid the highest, 5.

Suppose that the oxygen and nitrogen in the air were very much disposed to unite together, forming compounds. What would happen? Suppose, for example, that once in a while these gases should unite in the air and make a large quantity of laughing gas. In whatever country this should happen, all the people, men, women, and children, would be running about crazy, laughing, kissing, and playing all manner of strange pranks.

Or suppose that these gases should all at once unite to form nitric acid in the air. It would rain down upon the people, destroying the life of every animal and every plant, eating them, and thus make the earth desolate.

[illegible] the nitrogen and oxygen that are now in your lungs should [illegible] moment unite to form nitric acid, it would so irritate and [illegible] them that you would probably die instantly of suffocation. [illegible] the Creator has so made these gases that they can not [illegible] together when they are mixed, and the air is one of the [illegible] and pleasantest of all the mixtures that he has given us. [illegible] at the end of the creation, he pronounced all his works to [illegible] good," he meant the air as well as other things. It is [illegible] good—for all the purposes for which it is wanted.

God has made some things in such a way that they will unite together very readily. Thus you saw, in the experiments in which phosphorus was burned, on pages 20 and 25, that phosphorus unites with oxygen and forms phosphoric acid. Now, if phosphorus were diffused through the air in fine particles as nitrogen is, it would not do to have it unite so easily with oxygen. But there is none of it in the air, and it is present only in those places where it will not do harm, but good, to have it like the oxygen so well. This, and many other things that I shall tell you about, show that the Creator fits every thing exactly for the places it is to be in, the company that it is to keep, and the things that it is to do.

Questions.—Is air a compound? Give the comparison about alcohol and water. Of what is nitric acid composed? Why is it called *aqua fortis?* What is said of the difference between this and the gases that compose it? What of the difficulty of making these gases unite to form nitric acid? Tell about the effect of lightning upon them. Of what is the laughing gas composed? What are its effects when breathed? Why is it called laughing gas? What is said of its being a compound? What of the difference between this compound and nitric acid? What is the cause of this difference? How many compounds of oxygen and nitrogen are there? What are the proportions of oxygen in them? If the oxygen and nitrogen in the air were very ready to unite together, what effects would be produced? What would happen if the oxygen and nitrogen now in your lungs should all at once unite to form nitric acid? What is said about the creation of air? What about the readiness of phosphorus and oxygen to unite?

CHAPTER V.

CARBON.

...us far I have spoken of there being two gases in the mix... that we call air. But there is a third gas, in very small ...tity, in the air, called carbonic acid, or carbonic acid gas. ...is only one gallon of this gas in every 2500 gallons of air.

Fig. 10.

The proportions of the three gases in the air may be illustrated by Fig. 10. The largest square represents the nitrogen, the next the oxygen, and the very little one the carbonic acid. Although there is so small a proportion of this gas in the air, the little that there is has a very im... ...fluence, as you will soon see.

...acid gas differs from oxygen and nitrogen in being ...of two things. Oxygen is one thing, and so is nitro... ...ther of them can be in any way divided into two things. ...therefore called *elements*, or elementary substances. But ...acid is not an element, but a *compound*, for it is made of ...ngs *united together in one*. Observe that these two things ...mixed together as the two elements nitrogen and oxygen ...he air, but they are *united* together so as to make one thing ...as much one as if it were really an element. The two ...which compose carbonic acid are your lively friend that

you have become so well acquainted with, oxygen, and another that I will now introduce to your acquaintance, carbon.

Carbon appears in various forms, but the most common is that of charcoal. It is for this reason that the two names, charcoal and carbon, are ordinarily used by chemists as meaning the same thing. The various kinds of coal that we burn are mostly carbon. Plumbago, or black lead, as it is called, is a form of carbon. It is this which is used in our lead-pencils. The name black lead is very improper, for there is not a particle of lead in this substance. It is wholly carbon, with the exception of a very, very little iron which is generally present in it.

In the diamond we have carbon perfectly pure and beautifully crystallized. How strange that this most costly and brilliant of gems should be made of the same material with common dull and black charcoal! But so it is. And yet no man has ever discovered any way of changing charcoal into diamonds. The Creator alone knows how diamonds are made.

Diamonds are very expensive. Fifty dollars will buy but a small one. The largest one ever found is about the size of half a hen's egg. The famous one which now belongs to the Queen of England is less than half of the size of this, but it is valued at three millions of dollars.

Diamonds are commonly found in the sands of rivers, and there is generally gold with them. There are many diamonds found in Brazil. A few have been found in this country, mostly in North Carolina.

The diamond is the hardest substance in the world. You can not scratch a diamond with any thing else but another diamond;

... preparing a diamond to be set, it is ground with the powder of diamonds. The instrument with which the glazier cuts has a small diamond in its end.

The different forms of carbon can be burned. Most of them in common air; but black lead and the diamond will not. To burn them you must have oxygen alone, without any ni-

... what comes from this burning of carbon. You remember that in Chapter III. I told you that when phosphorus ... it unites with the oxygen of the air, making phosphoric ... which goes up in fumes. So, when carbon burns, it unites with oxygen, and forms carbonic acid gas. This gas is formed when we burn a diamond in oxygen, as well as when we burn charcoal. It is rather an expensive experiment to burn ... and it has not often been performed.

... charcoal that we use is, you know, made from wood. It ... is only partly burned. It is made by burning wood ... which is covered up with turf and dirt. There are ... openings left above and below, so that a little air ... among the wood, and thus keep up a smothered

... explanation is this. Wood is composed of carbon, united ... other things. Now what we want to do is to get the ... by itself. This we do by burning the wood just ... drive these other substances that are with the carbon ... off into the air. Some of the carbon is lost in this ... the oxygen unites with it, and they fly off together ... acid gas. But most of the carbon remains, and we have it in the shape of charcoal. In making charcoal it is necessary to take great care not to let in too much air, lest the fire should be too free, and burn out more of the carbon than is required. As there is always considerable water even in wood that seems to be very dry, this is driven off by the heat mingled with the smoke.

Fig. 11.

You can readily make charcoal in a small way. Take a test tube, *a*, Fig. 11, and hold a burning slip of wood, *b*, in it. The tube prevents the air from getting freely to the wood, and makes a smothered burning, and so you have a slender piece of charcoal.

Hard coal is almost wholly carbon. It differs from charcoal in being very solid. It is supposed that all the coal that man gets out of coal-mines was once wood. How, then, did it become coal? Man can not make such coal from wood; but God can do a great many things that man can not. But do we know how the Creator made this hard coal? We know something about it. We know that there must have been great heat and great pressure at the same time. While the wood was heated or partly burned, the rocks, we know not how high, were pressing down upon it, and so made the coal very solid.

Soot is mostly carbon. It forms in the chimney in this way. Most of the wood, in burning, has its carbon unite with the oxygen of the air, forming carbonic acid gas, which flies off. This gas you can not see any more than you can air. But the smoke of the fire you can see, so that there must be something in it besides carbonic acid. What you see is made up mostly of very fine particles of carbon which are thrown off from the burning wood and fly up the chimney. Many of these particles lodge on the chimney's sides in the form of soot.

When a lamp smokes because the wick is too high, the smoke is made up of these little particles of carbon, for there is carbon in oil as well as in wood. The reason that it smokes is that more carbon comes up the wick than is sufficient to unite with the oxygen that comes to it. If you could make the oxygen come to the wick faster, it would stop the smoking; for then there would be oxygen enough to turn all the carbon into carbonic acid gas. So, too, the smoking would stop if you should put the lamp into a jar of oxygen gas. There would, in that case, be five times as much oxygen all around the wick as there is when the lamp is in the air.

The lampblack so much used in painting is a kind of charcoal. It is made by letting the smoke of burning pitch or rosin into a sort of chamber lined with leather. In Fig. 12 you see the process represented. In the iron pot, *a*, some pitch or tar is made to boil, and the fumes pass into the chamber *b*, *c*, which is lined with leather. At *d* is a sort of hood, the height of which can be regulated by a pulley. This is to keep the fumes from passing upward too rapidly. The lampblack collects on the leathern sides of the chamber.

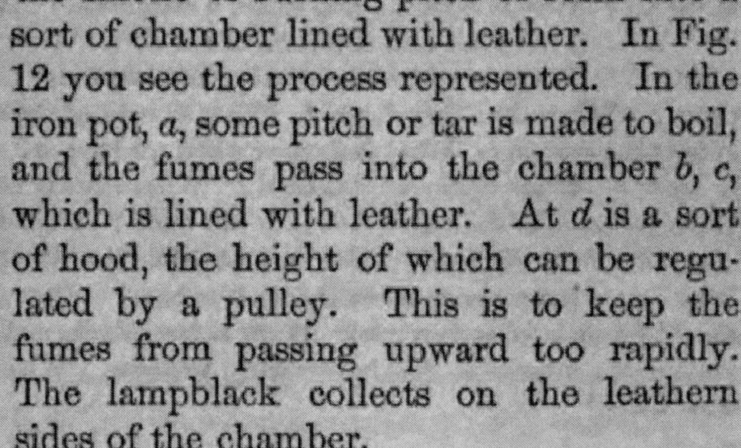
Fig. 12.

There is much carbon in many very different things that we see every where. There is carbon in chalk and marble. It is combined in these with oxygen and lime, so that it does not show itself as carbon any more than it does in carbonic acid gas. It is in egg-shells, oyster-shells, and in all shells. It is in all wood, as I have before told you, and makes an important part of all leaves, flowers, and fruit, and, indeed, of most vegetable substances. Your body, and the bodies of all animals, have carbon as one of its principal ingredients. But it does not show itself in them as carbon any more than it does in the white chalk and marble. It is hidden in them by being united with other things. By separating it from these things, it can be brought out from its concealment, and be shown as carbon, as you have seen that we do when we make charcoal from wood.

Questions.—How many gases are there in the air? How much carbonic acid gas is there in it? Explain Fig. 10. What is an element? What elements are there in the air? Why is carbonic acid called a compound? What are the two elements in it? What is the most common form of carbon? What is plumbago? What is the diamond? What is said of the making of diamonds? What of their size and expense? Where are they found? What is said of their hardness? What is said of burning carbon? What is formed when we burn it? How is charcoal commonly made? What is the explanation? What care is needed in making charcoal? What becomes of the water that is in the wood? Explain Fig. 11. How does hard coal differ from charcoal? How is it probable that it was made? Tell about soot. Why does a lamp smoke when the wick is high? Why would it stop smoking if you should put it into oxygen gas? What is lampblack, and how is it made? Mention some of the substances that have carbon in them. What is said about separating it from them?

CHAPTER VI.

CARBONIC ACID.

... acid gas, as you learned in the previous chapter, is ... of the solid carbon and the gas oxygen. The solid is no ... but is united with a gas to form a gas; and then ... formed is united with many substances to form ... for example, in chalk and marble we have this gas com... lime.

... can obtain carbonic acid from either of these sub... and marble, by putting with it something which ... the lime from it. An acid which we call muriatic ... this, because it has a greater liking or affinity for the ... carbonic acid has. If we pour, then, some of this ... glass vessel, and drop in some pieces of chalk or mar... get the carbonic acid gas away from the lime. An ... at once occurs. This is caused by the gas, which ... the chalk as the muriatic acid takes the lime away ... gas rises, and, pushing up the air before it, fills the ...

... want to know how much of the muriatic acid and the ... need to use in making the gas. If your glass jar ... pour into it two teaspoonsful of the acid. Then ... little bits of chalk till the effervescence ceases. In ... will get your jar full of the gas, the muriatic acid ... being united together in the bottom of it.

This is commonly spoken of as one of the ways of *making* gas: but this is hardly a proper expression. The gas is *made*: it is in the chalk, united with the lime, and we only se rate it from the lime by putting muriatic acid there to take lime away from it.

But there are ways of *making* this gas. For example, when burn charcoal in a jar of oxygen, as represented in Fig. 6, carbon unites with the oxygen in the burning, and we have the jar carbonic acid gas. Here we make the gas, for we ca the carbon to unite with the oxygen and thus form it.

So, also, we make carbonic acid if we burn charcoal in a jar common air. In such case, however, we do not get it alone, it has a large quantity of nitrogen mingled with it; you can how much, for you know what the proportion of nitrogen is in

Whenever, in fact, you set fire to any common thing in the wood, or a candle, or a bit of rag or paper, you set a going manufacture of carbonic acid gas. There is carbon in all th things, and in the burning it unites with the oxygen of the and forms carbonic acid.

For most of the experiments that we want to try with carbo acid, it answers to obtain it in the way that I first mentione but for some experiments it will not do to have any thing left the bottom of the jar. In that case the gas must made in a retort or a flask, and so pass out and collected in jars, as you remember we obtain oxyg gas. Or, we can obtain it in the way represented Fig. 18. Here you see a flask containing the cha and the muriatic acid. A bent tube is fastened into the cork

Fig. 18.

one end, and the other end is at the bottom of the jar in which we want to collect the gas. Now observe the operation. There is air in both the flask and the jar. This is driven out by the gas as it forms. This gas is considerably heavier than air, and so the air in the jar very readily passes out, and leaves the jar full of the gas.

Let us look, now, at some of the qualities of carbonic acid gas. It has no color, and is transparent. In these respects it is like oxygen and nitrogen. It has a faint smell and a slightly acid taste.

Nothing will burn in this gas. If you lower a candle into a jar of it, it will go out. A very pretty experiment is sometimes tried, showing how different this gas is from oxygen in this respect. We have two jars, one full of oxygen, and the other of carbonic acid. If the candle be lowered into the jar of carbonic acid, it goes out. If, now, we instantly put it into the jar of oxygen, the spark of fire on the wick lights up at once into a bright flame. And so we can pass the candle back and forth several times, putting it out and relighting it each time.

Why does the candle go out in the carbonic acid? Because there is no oxygen there to make it burn. But perhaps you will say that there is oxygen there, for carbonic acid is composed of oxygen and carbon. True; but the oxygen is not there as oxygen, for it is united with the carbon so as to make something entirely different. The union is a close one. The carbon clings, as we may say, to the oxygen, and will not let it go to the burning candle.

As nothing can burn in this gas, so no animal can live in it. Put a mouse into a jar of it, and he will die at once. I have told you that there is a little of this gas in common air, but it is so very little that it does no harm to us and to other animals.

Carbonic acid gas is much heavier than air. You can therefore pour it, like water, from one vessel into another. Of course the vessel into which you pour it is full of air. What becomes, then, of the air? It rises and goes out of the vessel, just as oil would if you should pour water into a vessel filled with it.

Fig. 14.

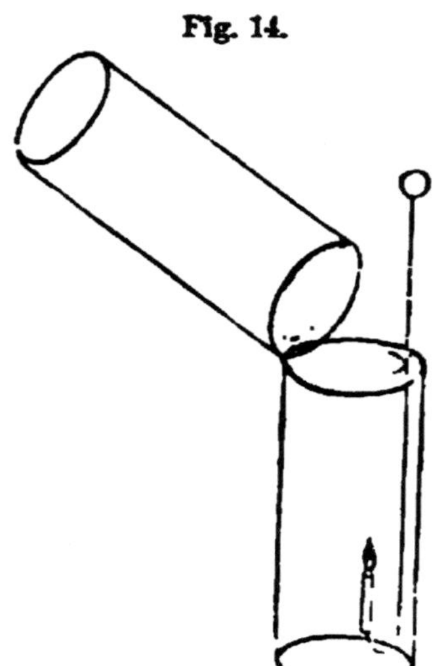

Suppose, as represented in Fig. 14, you have a lighted taper in a jar of common air, and hold a jar of carbonic acid gas over it, as you see there; the gas will go down into the lower jar, forcing up the air, and put out the light.

In Fig. 15 is represented a very pretty experiment, which shows that this gas is heavier than air. In the first place, you balance a jar by a weight. I say balance a jar. Is that exactly correct? Is there not something in the jar? "No," you will perhaps say, "it is empty." But think a moment. That jar is full of something, and that something has weight. It is full of air. You have balanced, then, a jar full

Fig. 15.

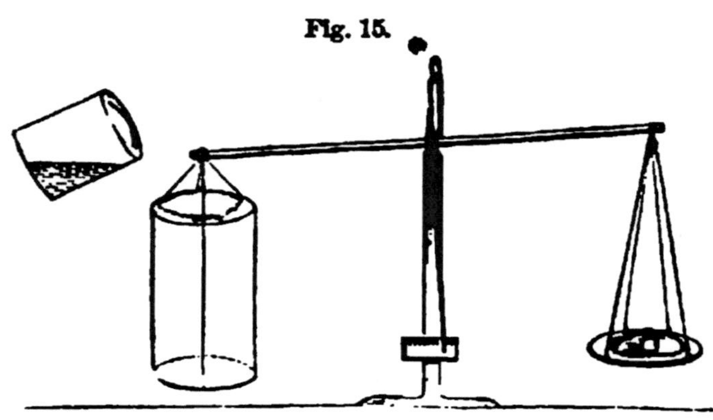

air. Now if, as represented, some carbonic acid gas be poured wn into the jar on the scales, the jar will fall and the weight will rise. Why? Because there is now a gas in the jar that is heavier than air.

Fig. 16.

If you have a jar filled with this gas, you can take it out with a little bucket, as seen in Fig. 16. As you take one bucketful after another out, you can pour it away as you would water; and the air will go into the jar to take the place of the gas as fast as you remove it.

If you blow a soap-bubble and let it fall into a jar full of carbonic acid gas, it will not go to the bottom of the jar and break, as it would if the jar were full of air. It will fall down a little into the jar, and then go back and remain in its open mouth. Why is this? The air that u have blown into the bubble is lighter than the gas in the jar, d the bubble therefore floats on the surface of the gas as a boat ats on the surface of water. If the jar be only half full of the s, air filling, therefore, the upper half, the bubble will stop half y down in the jar, and there remain.

Questions.—What is said of the formation of carbonic acid gas? What is the nposition of chalk and marble? How can we get the carbonic acid from them? you wish to make a quart of carbonic acid gas, how would you do it? Explain . 13. How is carbonic acid like oxygen and nitrogen? What are its taste and ell? Give the experiment with the two jars of gases. Why does the candle go t in the carbonic acid? What is said of the union of oxygen with carbon in this s? How about living in carbonic acid? What is said of the weight of this gas? plain Fig. 14. Give the experiment represented in Fig. 16. Describe and exin the experiment with the soap-bubble.

CHAPTER VII.

CARBONIC ACID—*Continued.*

A VERY entertaining experiment, showing that carbonic gas is heavier thar is represented in Fi The gas is poured upon a row of li candles, putting ou after another.

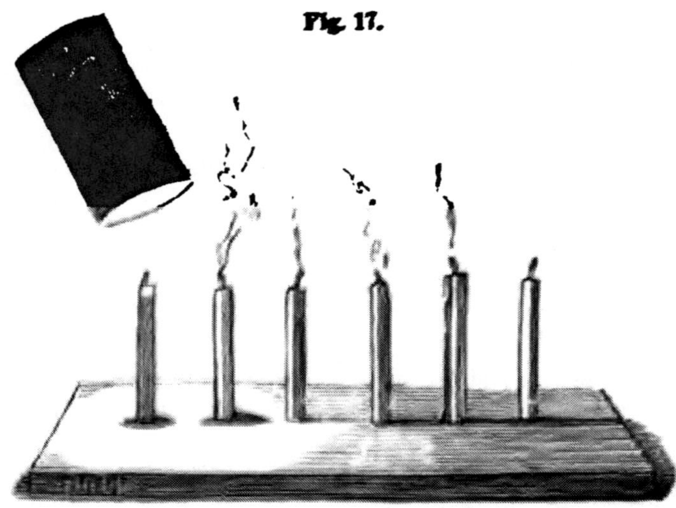

Fig. 17.

This gas has beer to put out fire. years ago a fire beg a coal-mine in Sco and burned away a a rate that it could r put out by any common means, and the mine could no long worked. There was danger that a large amount of coal wou consumed if the fire continued long. A Mr. Gurney contriv some way to make a great quantity of carbonic acid gas in a of the mine where it would sink down to the fire, and put i

As carbonic acid gas is so heavy, it is apt to remain belo wherever it collects. It sometimes is produced in conside quantity in wells. When this is the case it remains at the tom of the well. Suppose a man goes down into such a w clean it; he will have no difficulty at first, because the good; that is, it has enough of oxygen in it, and not too much of carbonic acid. But when he gets near the bottom, where the carbonic acid gas has accumulated, he gasps for breath, and falls. Perhaps some one, not understanding the cause of the trouble, goes down to relieve the man, and he also falls senseless. Many lives have been lost in this way.

Now how can we find out whether this gas has collected in a well? Let a light down. If it goes out, there is a good deal of the gas there; and if it burns dimly when it comes near the bottom, there is enough of the gas to make it dangerous. A very good way is for the man who goes down a well to take a candle with him, as you see in Fig. 18. He must hold the candle considerably below his mouth, or it will do no good. If his light goes out, or becomes quite dim, he must stop at once, for another step would bring his mouth down into the gas, so that he would take it into his lungs.

Fig. 18.

Now the question comes, when there is some of this gas in a well or pit, how can we get rid of it, so that it may be safe for a man to go down into the well? There are several expedients for this. One is to let down a bucket a good many times, turning it each time upside down in the air to let the gas fall out. This will remind the experiment represented in Fig. 16.

But this will not get all the gas out. Well, another ex is to let down a bundle of straw or shavings on fire. Th the gas, and so makes it lighter; and, therefore, if the bu held to one side of the well, the heated gas will pass up th

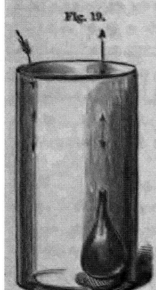

Fig. 19.

while cool good air will go down the take its place. The manner in which erates can be illustrated by the experi Fig. 19. In a jar of carbonic acid gas placed a flask full of hot water, and cork rests on a pad, to keep it in its place side of the jar. This heats the gas all ar and there is, therefore, an upward current side of the jar, while there is a downw rent of cool good air at the other side. currents are indicated by the arrows. gas is driven out can be shown by letting ed taper down into the jar. If it is all g taper will burn as brightly as when it is

Another expedient is to throw some slaked lime, mix water, down the sides of the well. Observe how this o You remember that chalk is composed of carbonic acid a Now there is the carbonic acid in the well, and if you lime there, so that this gas can get at it, they will unite and form chalk. This is the object of having the mixture and water drip down the sides of the well. The gas uni the lime, and so chalk is formed, and sticks to the stones dry lime were thrown down it would pass the gas, and be lodged in the water below where get at it.

as I have before told you, some carbonic acid but it is mixed up with the nitrogen and oxygen. mixed with them? As it is heavier than these it not lie all along close to the earth with these water lies under the lighter oil when they are in a It is because gases are so ready to mingle to- motion will make them do it at once, and you there is always motion in the air. Even when it ap- still there is some motion, as you may know by the you see flying about in the air in a still room as the in reveal them to your view.

together as spirits of wine and water do. They from oil and water in this respect. You may water, and yet they will not mingle. The water shaking is over, take its place below the oil. But of wine, or any kind of liquor, shaken together, and stay mixed. So it is with the gases the air.

some alcohol or spirits of wine very carefully into filled with water, the water, which is heavier than will remain at the bottom. Just so the carbonic acid heavier than the air, will remain very quietly at the well when it is formed there. It is because the air in so still. If you could shake up the air and the car- you can the alcohol and water, you could make together.

See now what would happen if carbonic acid gas did no gle with the other gases of the air. Being heavier than the it would get below them, as water gets below air. It would a sea of gas over the sea of water, covering all the valleys plains. You see what would be the consequence to us and o animals. No animal, small or great, could live any where ex on hills and mountains, for there only could he find any oxyg to breathe.

There are some places on the earth where carbonic acid colle in large quantities. There is such a place in Italy, called Grotto del Cane, or Dog's Grotto. The reason of this name will soon see. On the floor of this grotto or cave there is alwa a layer of this gas. The layer is high enough to reach above head of a dog, but not the head of a man. A man lives near who shows the grotto to visitors, and, in doing this, he takes dog in, who of course falls down senseless. He brings him, however, quickly into the fresh air, which, with a dash of water, revives the dog, so that the same thing can be shown the next visitors. But you can see by his leanness and the ness of his eye that he is dealt with hardly; for this gas, un nitrogen, is really poisonous. The dog falls senseless not mere for want of oxygen, but because the gas does him positive harm

Where do you think the gas in this grotto comes from? comes out from crevices in the rocks, being made somewhere the earth near by. It is not uncommon for it to come out fro such crevices and from cracks in the earth, and sometimes it bu

* To realize this difference between this gas and nitrogen, turn back to what I s about nitrogen on page 28.

bles up through the water of springs in the neighborhood of volcanoes. Generally, however, it flies off in the air. Why, then, does it collect in this grotto? It is because it is so much shut in that the air does not circulate freely, and so some of the gas remains on the floor of the cave.

The operation of the Grotto del Cane can be illustrated by a simple arrangement represented in Fig. 20. We have here a box with pasteboard, A B B, fastened all around the edges, variously cut and painted so as to represent rocks. The lower edge must, of course, have a piece of the pasteboard, A, to keep the gas from going out there. A hole is made on the top through which the taper can be let down into the imitation grotto. There is also a hole in the side for the pipe that brings the gas in from the bottle, C. If you remember what I told you about obtaining carbonic acid gas, you can tell what is in that bottle. On looking at this arrangement, you readily see that, as the air in the box is still, the heavy gas will quickly collect on the floor, being prevented

Fig. 20.

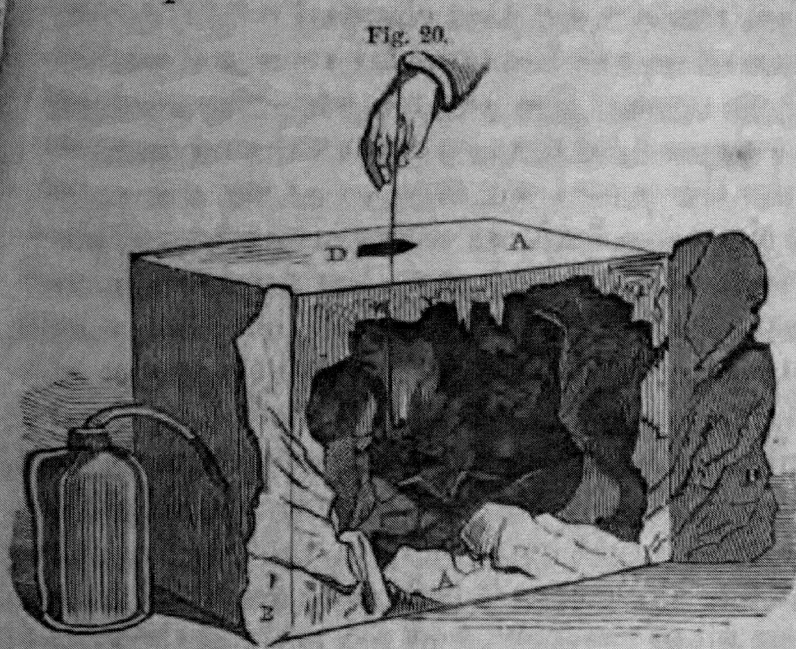

CHAPTER VIII.

THE AIR.

I HAVE already told you much about the air, but we will consider its composition more particularly.

You have learned much about the three gases of which it is composed. The largest part of the air is nitrogen, there is about four times as much of it as there is of the oxygen. Of carbonic acid there is a very small proportion, as you realize by looking at the figure on page 31. Yet there is really a great quantity of this gas in the whole of the air, for you must remember that the atmosphere is 45 or 50 miles high. It is calculated that over every acre of land there are seven tons of carbonic acid gas.

There are continual additions made to the carbonic acid in the air in various ways. Every fire or light that burns adds to it; for, as you learned in Chapters V. and VI., the burning carbon of wood and other substances unites with the oxygen of the air and forms carbonic acid gas, which flies off.

You see that the fire or light lessens the oxygen of the air at the same time that it adds to the carbonic acid. If you put a candle under a glass jar placed on a smooth plate with its open end downward, it will burn brightly at first, because there is enough oxygen in the air inclosed in the jar; but soon it will burn dimly, and, after a while, go out. The reason is that the carbon of the candle uses up the oxygen by uniting with it to form carbo

the candle is about to go out, you lift up the ... the candle will brighten up again, because you ... the carbonic acid, and the fresh air that comes in ... candle with oxygen.

... that all fires and lights lessen the oxygen in the ... carbonic acid.

... every animal is breathing out carbonic acid from its ... you can prove in your own case by a simple experi... a tumbler or bowl some lime water. With a ... this, and you will find, after a little time, that ... become quite milky. The reason is that the ... which came out from your lungs has united with ... lime water, and formed carbonate of lime, or ... standing a little while the water will become clear, ... settled at the bottom in a fine powder. This ... I presume, of another instance mentioned before, ... carbonic acid were introduced to each other so ... unite. I refer to one of the expedients for get... the carbonic acid in it. Try to recollect it; but, ... to it on page 44.

... of carbonic acid which we breathe out in twenty... considerable. It is calculated that a full-grown ... in twenty-four hours over two pounds of car... this there is over half a pound of solid carbon ... throws off, therefore, from his lungs, in the ... nearly 200 pounds of charcoal—considerably ... weight, even if he be quite a large-sized man.

... of every size, from the elephant down to the

animals that are not small you can see breathe—you can see the chest move; but in the very largest leaves that you can find, the leaves of corn or the pumpkin vine, you never see any motion in the breathing. They are very still in their breathing. But the greatest difference is in another thing. While lungs, in breathing, give out carbonic acid, the leaves take it in; and while lungs take in oxygen, the leaves give it out. Every leaf that you see gleaming in the sun is busy pouring out into the air oxygen from all its little pores, and taking in, at the same time, carbonic acid gas.

I have told you what becomes of the oxygen that is absorbed by the blood in the lungs; but what becomes of the carbonic acid which the leaves absorb? This furnishes carbon for the growth of the plant. You learned in Chapter V. that carbon is one of the chief ingredients of wood. Now a very large part of this carbon is taken in by the pores, or little open mouths, of the leaves. These are spread out like nets to catch the carbon floating in the air in the carbonic acid gas, and this is carried to all parts of the plant to help it grow. Whenever you are looking, then, at a large tree, just think how a great part of that solid wood was once moving about in the air, and was caught up by millions upon millions of little mouths in thousands upon thousands of outspread leaves. Think, too, that perhaps some of that hard wood was once in your soft breath coming out from your lungs. Even the little insect that hums among its leaves may have furnished some, a little, of the carbon which is in the tree.

The carbon which you breathe out from your lungs is scattered about, and goes to leaves far and near. But suppose it were

...alone, how much carbon do you think your ... the trees in a year? More than the weight ... and that would be enough to make quite a ...

... that there is a regular exchange going on be... lungs every where; lungs give carbon to leaves, ... oxygen in exchange. But how is this in winter, ... no leaves except upon the evergreens? Do these ... all the carbon that is breathed out then? No, ... enough of them to do this. Does the carbonic acid ... the air, and the oxygen lessen? Not at all. It ... as it is in summer, when the leaves are all alive and ... will tell you how this is. You remember how I ... the gases were very ready to mix up with each oth... when they are shaken together. Now every motion ... gust of wind, shakes up the gases that compose ... the carbonic acid gas that arises any where ... This gas therefore, we may say, flies on the ... and, breathed out in one place, it may thus ... many places, not merely miles, but thousands of ... That which is breathed out at the north in winter ... south to be drank up by leaves there, while these ... up oxygen for the lungs of the north.

... the carbonic acid in the air, you see, are contin... The oxygen is constantly used up by being ab... and by uniting with substances that are burning. ... fresh oxygen is poured forth from the leaves of ... the air; so also the carbonic acid is continually changing, being absorbed by the leaves, while new carbonic acid is supplied from the lungs of all animals, from fires and lights, etc.

Now in the midst of this change the air in all parts of the earth has always exactly the same proportions of the three gases. If a gallon of air from Europe, and another from Asia, and another from Africa were brought here and examined by a chemist, he would find that each of them had the same amounts of nitrogen, and oxygen, and carbonic acid that a gallon of American air has. How wonderful this is! In this exchange which is going on between the leaves on the one hand, and lungs, fires, and lights on the other, how is this balance so nicely kept? We do not know; but the Creator understands it, and he has all power, and so secures this regularity even in so changing a thing as air.

But what I have just said about the air is true only of that which is out of doors, free to go "where it listeth." When it is shut up the proportions of its ingredients may be very much changed. Suppose there are a great many persons crowded in a small close room; their lungs are using up the oxygen and pouring out carbonic acid gas. A little fresh air gets in at cracks and loose places about the windows and doors, but this is not enough to prevent the air in the room from losing a great deal of its oxygen, and becoming loaded with carbonic acid. For this reason, the lights, after a while, burn dimly, and the people become dull and drowsy. A gallon of air taken from this room at such a time would be very different from a gallon taken from the air outside. It would have just as much nitrogen in it, but much less of the life-giving oxygen, and much more of the poisonous carbonic acid.

[illegible] of life by want of ventilation.

[illegible] what happens when the doors of such a room are [illegible] the people go out. The carbonic acid flies off at once [illegible] far and wide, to be drank up by the mouths in [illegible] and the fresh air rushes in to supply its place.

[illegible] is done to the health of people by breathing air [illegible] with carbonic acid. It may not be felt much at [illegible] such air be breathed often, a little harm done each [illegible] a while, amount to a great deal. A few persons [illegible] killed on board of the Londonderry, but a multi-[illegible] are killed every year by breathing bad air in rooms, [illegible] do not know it, because it is done so slowly.

[illegible] the gases in the air? What is said of the quantity of car-[illegible] What effect have fires and lights upon the carbonic acid of [illegible] its oxygen? How does a candle burning under a glass jar [illegible] How does the breathing of animals affect the carbonic acid of the [illegible] experiment with lime water. How is this like one of the expedients [illegible] acid from a well? What is said of the quantity of carbon [illegible] lungs? What of the supply of carbonic acid to the air from [illegible] What is said of the taking in of oxygen by the lungs? [illegible] by drowning? How does the air which we breathe out differ [illegible] Give the experiment with the mouse. State the compari-[illegible] Tell the story of the emigrant ship. How does the air con-[illegible] same quantity of carbonic acid and oxygen? What is said of the [illegible] What is done with the carbonic acid which the leaves ab-[illegible] do you give to the leaves? What is said of the exchange [illegible] How is it with this exchange in winter? What is said [illegible] in the carbonic acid and the oxygen of the air? What is [illegible] of uniformity in the midst of this change? What is said of [illegible] containing many persons? What is done with this air when [illegible] and the people go out? What is said of the injury to health [illegible] air?

CHAPTER IX.

HYDROGEN.

WATER is composed of two gases. One of these is oxygen, which you have learned so much in previous chapters; the oth is hydrogen. This is the lightest of all gases, and therefore t lightest of all substances. Air is fifteen times as heavy as hyd gen. A balloon, therefore, filled with this gas goes up very sw ly in the air.

As hydrogen is the lightest of all substances, a metal called p tinum is the heaviest. F 21 exhibits the comparat weights of four substanc platinum, water, air, and h drogen. The little shot platinum equals in wei the balls or spheres of w ter, air, and hydrogen rep sented in the figure.

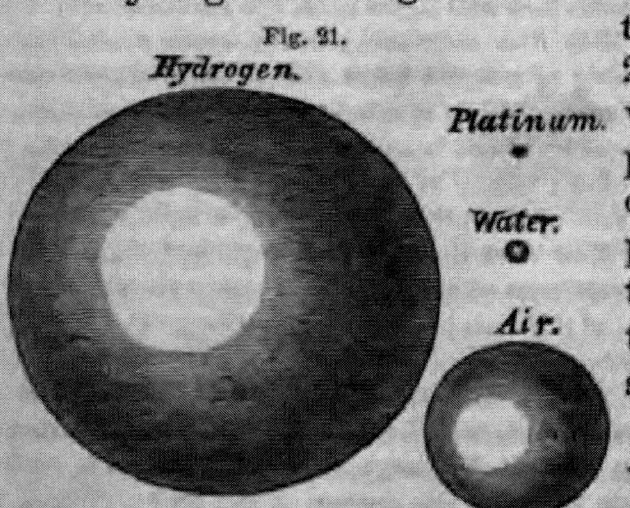

Fig. 21.

In every nine pounds water there are eight of ygen gas and only one hydrogen. But as oxygen is sixteen times as heavy as hyd gen, the bulk of the hydrogen that goes to form any portion water is twice as great as that of the oxygen in it. This may represented by Fig. 22. The smaller space represents the oxygen. It is divided into eight spaces to represent the eight pounds. Now as hydrogen is only one sixteenth the weight of the same bulk of oxygen, it will take sixteen such spaces to represent the one pound of hydrogen, and this will make a figure containing twice the space of that representing the eight pounds of oxygen.

Fig. 22.

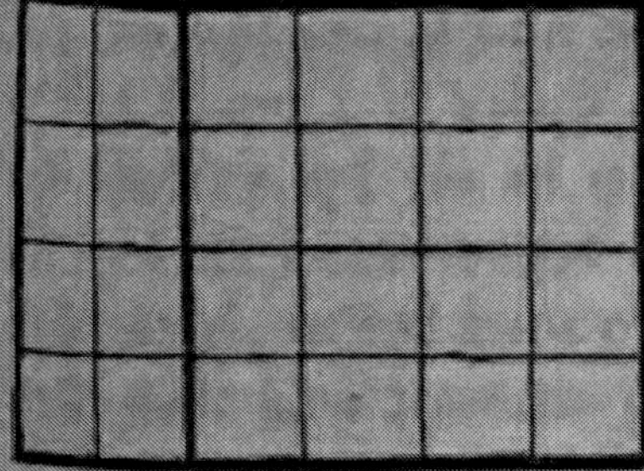

Hydrogen will burn with a brisk but faint flame, giving but little light. How strange it seems that oxygen, that makes other things burn, and hydrogen, a gas that itself burns, united together, form a liquid that puts out fire!

What will seem stranger still to you is that, when hydrogen gas is burned in oxygen, water is formed. In the burning, the oxygen and the hydrogen unite together. Not a jot of either of them is lost, just as none of the carbon and oxygen are lost when carbon is burned in oxygen; they merely go into a new condition, uniting to form a liquid. In doing this, the bulk of both of them is made much smaller. It takes a great deal of these gases to form a very small amount of water. You will realize this by looking at Fig. 21, remembering that oxygen is nearly of the same weight with air. It will take, of hydrogen and oxygen mingled together, an amount only a little less than that representing hydrogen in the figure to make a drop of water of the size represented.

If hydrogen be burned in air, we have the same result as when it is burned in oxygen. The hydrogen unites with the oxygen of the air and forms water. It will have nothing to do with the nitrogen that is in the air, but lets it alone, and takes the oxygen and combines with it. You can see that water is formed by the burning of hydrogen in air by various experiments. One is represented in Fig. 23. This figure you have seen before, in the first chapter, and the experiment was then partly explained. You are now prepared to understand a fuller explanation of it. There are carbon and hydrogen united together in the tallow. Yes, this lightest of all the gases helps, in this case, to form a solid substance. As the melted tallow goes up the wick, the air brings oxygen to it all around, and the heat makes this oxygen unite with both the carbon and hydrogen of the tallow. By uniting with the carbon it forms carbonic acid. This is, you know, a colorless transparent gas, and so you do not see it. But there it is in the jar. Uniting with the hydrogen, the oxygen forms water. This goes up in vapor with the carbonic acid, and so also you do not see that. But this vapor soon collects on the inside of the glass, because it is cool. The glass therefore becomes dim, and after a little time there is enough water there to form drops and trickle down into the plate.

Fig. 23.

In Fig. 24 you have another experiment. Here hydrogen alone is burned without carbon. The bottle that you see contains the materials for making the gas, of which I will tell you soon. The flame of the hydrogen passes into the horn-shaped glass. The va-

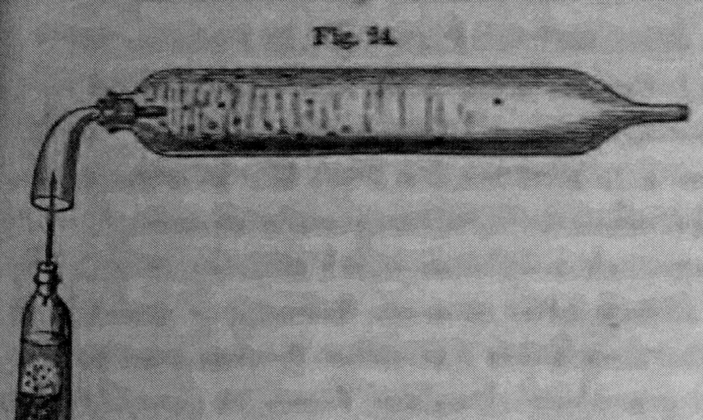
Fig. 24.

por formed there by the union of the hydrogen with the oxygen of the air passes into that long glass vessel, and there is condensed, as you see, in drops.

You see how ready oxygen is to unite with hydrogen. But you remember that, in a previous chapter, I have told you that the oxygen and nitrogen in the air would not unite, however much they were heated and shaken together; nothing but lightning can make them unite. You see one reason for this difference. If the oxygen and nitrogen in the air could be easily made to unite, very bad effects would be experienced, as I told you in Chapter III. But when oxygen unites with hydrogen the result is water, which will do no harm. Water we want in abundance. We want it in the air as well as every where else, for dry air would be very uncomfortable and injurious to us. It is the water in the air, in the form of unseen vapor, that makes the air so soft and pleasant to us. But nitric acid, and the other compounds of oxygen and nitrogen, we do not want in the air, and if much of them were there they would destroy every living thing.

I will now tell you how hydrogen is obtained. We put into a retort, or a bottle, some bits of zinc, some water, and a little sulphuric acid, which is commonly called oil of vitriol. Now the acid makes the oxygen of the water unite with the zinc, and the hydrogen of the water is therefore set free. This rises and passes out of the vessel, carrying the air that is in the vessel along with it; and soon, when all the air is driven out, the gas comes out alone. In Fig. 25 is represented what is called the "philosopher's candle." The zinc, water, and sulphuric acid are in the bottle, which is fitted with a cork having a tube in it. The gas issuing from the tube burns just as illuminating gas does issuing from a gas-burner. There is some caution required in making this gas in this way, for a mixture of it with common air is explosive. If, therefore, you should hold a light to the tube before the air is driven out, you might have an explosion, and your bottle might be broken and its contents scattered about.

Fig. 25.

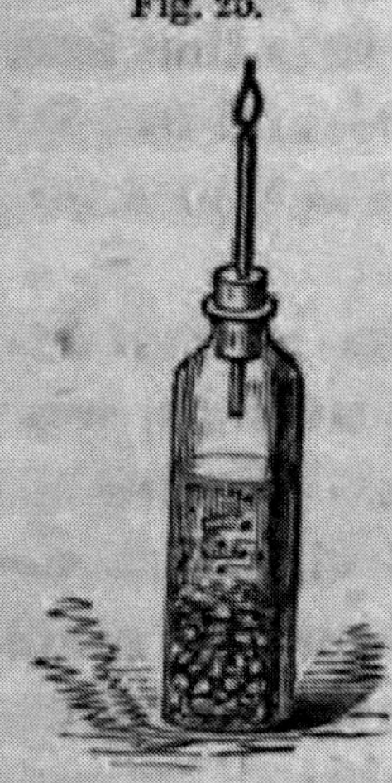

One way in which hydrogen is obtained shows how well oxygen likes iron. The apparatus is represented in Fig. 26. You see a furnace, C, with an iron pipe, B B, running through it, like a gun-barrel. In this pipe are put fine scrapings of iron or bits of needles. At one end of this pipe is another pipe from a flask of water, A, and the water is heated by a spirit-lamp under the flask. As the water boils, steam passes through the iron pipe in

Fig. 26.

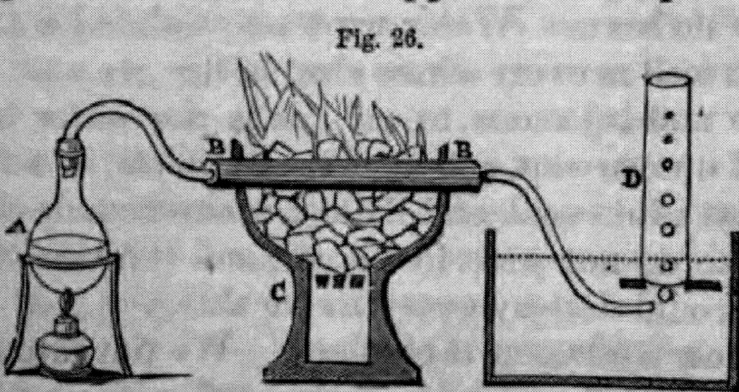

the furnace. Now steam is water, but very finely divided up, as we may say. As it passes through the red-hot pipe among the turnings of iron, the oxygen of the water is made by the heat to unite with the iron, and form rust. It parts company, therefore, with the hydrogen of the water, and so the hydrogen goes out alone through the other end of the pipe. You see it passing into the glass jar, D, in the pneumatic cistern.

You remember what I said about pouring carbonic acid gas downward. You can not do this with hydrogen. It is so light that, the moment it escapes from a vessel, it passes directly and quickly upward. You can let a jar of carbonic acid gas stand, and the gas will not go out; but if you set down a jar of hydrogen gas with its mouth upward, the gas will at once pass out, the air coming in to take its place. If you want to pour hydrogen gas from one jar into another, you must hold them in the manner represented in Fig. 27, the upper jar being the one which is to receive the gas.

Fig. 27.

I will make some comparisons between liquids and gases in these respects. If you should set a jar filled with the liquid metal mercury all over in water, the mercury would remain in the jar, for the same reason that carbonic acid does not rise out of the jar when left to stand in the air. As the carbonic acid is heavier than air, so is the mercury heavier than water. On the other hand, if you introduce a jar of oil into water, the oil will go up out of the jar, the water taking its place, as hydrogen gas goes up out of a jar set down in air, the air going in to take its place.

hot gas and vapor that come up from the light are confined in the chimney instead of spreading out in the air around; they pass up, therefore, very rapidly through the chimney, and so make a strong draught,* as we say. This makes the air come rapidly to the light from below, and of course a great deal of oxygen comes to it in a little time.

You see how great the draught is if you hold your hand over the top of the chimney; you will feel a current of hot gas and vapor striking against it. You must be careful not to put your hand too near. This current does not all of it go straight up, but it spreads out as soon as it escapes from the chimney, so that, at a little distance, your hand feels only a small part of the current, and that is somewhat cooled.

Another contrivance is to have the wick flat instead of round. You see that such a wick presents a larger surface to the air than a round one, and therefore more of it can be reached by the oxygen.

Some wicks are made circular, the air being admitted on the inside as well as the outside of the circle. A very bright light is made in this way.

Observe now how we start a fire. Commonly we do it by putting something burning to the combustible substance. Thus we set fire to wood by burning paper or shavings. So, as we open a gas-burner, we put to it a burning match, and thus set fire to the stream of gas as it comes out. But think a moment what sets fire to the match. It is rubbing it, you will say. But how?

* The manner in which this draught is produced is explained fully in the chapters on Heated Air and Chimneys, in the Third Part of the Child's Book of Nature.

The friction creates heat enough to cause the oxygen to unite with the phosphorus, and the union is quick enough to make light as well as heat. So you see that it is heat that causes what we call fire.

You can see this very often in kindling a wood fire. Suppose you have a bed of coals underneath the wood which is placed on the andirons, how is the wood set on fire? The coals heat the wood, and, after a little time, they make the wood hot enough to set it on fire. Here no flame goes from the coals to the wood, but only heat.

Now why is it that some substances take fire so much more easily than others? Why, for example, does a match with phosphorus on its end take fire by friction, while one dipped in sulphur will not, but must have fire touched to it? It is because the phosphorus has a greater liking or affinity for oxygen than sulphur, and therefore it requires less heat to make them unite. So charcoal has an affinity for oxygen, but not so much that you can make them unite by rubbing the charcoal. Phosphorus has a greater affinity for oxygen than any of the substances that I have yet told you about; it therefore takes fire so easily that you have to be very careful in handling it. But in another chapter I shall tell you about a substance, a metal, that likes oxygen so well that, if you put it into water, it will steal the oxygen from the hydrogen and unite with it, and the union is so quick that it sets the hydrogen all ablaze.

There are some substances that can not be burned at all. Gold is one of them. Iron, you have seen, can be burned; that is, it can be made to unite with oxygen; but you may expose gold to the hottest fire that you can make, and it will only melt. It will not burn. It will not unite with the oxygen that is all around it. It has no liking or affinity for oxygen, as iron has. And what is true of these two metals in regard to quick combustion, is also true of them in regard to the slow combustion that I spoke of in the first part of this chapter. Gold never rusts in the air; that is, it does not burn up with a slow fire, as iron does.

Questions.—What occurs usually in what we call combustion? Illustrate the difference between quick and slow combustion. Why are iron fences painted? How does water put out fire? Why does not the oxygen that is in the water make the fire burn? What is said of putting out fires by other means besides water? Give the conversation related about putting out fire. Explain the effect of blowing a fire with bellows. What would be the effect if you should blow nitrogen or carbonic acid upon a fire? Explain the operation of a glass chimney on a lamp. If you hold your hand over the top of the chimney, what strikes against it? What is the advantage of a flat wick? What of a circular one? When we set fire to any thing, what is it that starts the fire? Give the illustration of the match; also of the wood set fire by coals. Tell what affinity has to do with producing fire. What is said about the affinity of phosphorus for oxygen? What about the affinity of a certain metal for it?

CHAPTER XI.

GAS-MAKING AND GAS-BURNING.

EVERY candle or lamp is a gas factory. I will show you how this is in the common candle.

I have told you that there are both carbon and hydrogen in the tallow. They are united together there as a solid compound; but, as the candle burns, this solid becomes by the heat a liquid at the foot of the exposed part of the wick. See what a cup of melted tallow we have there. It is curious to observe how this cup is formed, and kept just so, all the time that the candle is burning away. The heat of the burning wick melts the tallow, but that which is nearest the wick is of course melted first. This keeps a raised edge all around. If the wick gets bent over to one side, it is apt to melt this edge on that side, and so some of the melted tallow runs out of the cup and down the side of the candle.

But the melted tallow at the foot of the wick must go up the wick to be burned. How is this? It goes up because there is an attraction between the wick and the liquid, and therefore the particles of the liquid go up every where among the fibres of the wick. This kind of attraction is commonly called *capillary* attraction, because it was first particularly observed on putting the ends of very small tubes in water, or almost any liquid. The smaller the tube was, the higher the liquid was observed to go up in it. The small tubes were called capillary tubes because

even take it away from the hydrogen in water, although [illegible] gen and oxygen are very strongly united [illegible]

Iron-rust is an *oxyd* of iron. It is so called [illegible] gen and iron united together. So the iron, when rusted, [illegible] to be *oxydized*. In like manner, potash is an oxyd of [illegible]

What is very commonly called potash is really [illegible] with carbonic acid, and of this I will tell you in another [illegible] What the chemist calls potash, that is, the oxyd of [illegible] a powerful substance. It will, like the strong acids, [illegible] and sulphuric, eat flesh, and so is called a caustic.

As potash is an oxyd of potassium, so soda is an oxyd [illegible] metal called sodium. This metal will swim on water like [illegible] sium. When thrown upon water it decomposes it, taking [illegible] oxygen from the hydrogen, as the potassium does. A [illegible] sound is produced, but the escaping hydrogen does not burn [illegible] less the water be hot. When it does burn the flame has a [illegible] tiful yellow color, which is given to it by the fumes of the [illegible]

There are great quantities of this metal in the world, for [illegible] one of the ingredients of common salt. But, like potassium, [illegible] never found alone by itself. It is always united with oxygen [illegible] some other substance.

Potash and soda are called *alkalies*. They have an acrid [illegible] the very opposite of that of acids. There is one substance, am-monia, which is called volatile alkali, because it is so ready to [illegible] off into the air, volatile coming from the Latin word *volo*, to fly. Potash and soda are sometimes termed *fixed* alkalies, in [illegible] tion from the ammonia, because they have no disposition to [illegible] [illegible] or are fixed to the spot where they are.

[illegible] gas, and is very pungent. Its compo- [illegible]. It is composed of nitrogen and hydrogen. [illegible] carbonic acid gas, the smelling salts with which [illegible].

[illegible] supposed to be a simple substance or element before [illegible] of Sir Humphrey Davy. But this, like soda and [illegible] found to be an oxyd of a metal. This metal, called [illegible] very difficult to obtain, because it has so great an [illegible] oxygen. It is hard to get calcium out of the company [illegible] oxygen long enough to let us see it. When it is [illegible] like silver. United with oxygen, calcium forms [illegible] is commonly called quick-lime. If water be added [illegible] called slaked lime. Observe that word *slaked*. Peo- [illegible] speak of slaking the thirst; so, in the case of lime, [illegible], as we may say, for water, and the lime will take [illegible] great deal of it. But there is a certain amount that [illegible] no more. When it has got that amount its af- [illegible], or its thirst is slaked. So it is called slaked [illegible]

[illegible] become slaked after a while if it be merely exposed [illegible] has such an affinity for water that it will drink in [illegible] from the air.

[illegible] mortar the lime is slaked; and so great is the af- [illegible] and water for each other, so eager are they to unite [illegible] great commotion and heat are produced, as you [illegible] often witnessed where building is going on.

[illegible] is dry, and yet in every four pounds of it there is [illegible] of water. This is about the same proportion that

to give the required hardness. Very commonly this is copper. Sometimes tin is used in place of lead. This makes a better though more expensive type-metal. Sometimes type-metal is made of zinc, copper, lead, and tin together. In the best type-metal there is some bismuth, which gives a good clear letter in printing. If you examine printed letters with a magnifying-glass, you will see great differences in the specimens, according to the kind of types used, and the length of time that they have been in use. You will be surprised to find how imperfect the letters are in their filling up in the very best of printing.

Bronze is an alloy of copper with tin, the tin being to the copper as about one to nine. This, you know, is much used in making statues and smaller ornamental figures. Bell-metal is a kind of bronze, having more tin in it than ordinary bronze.

Pewter is an alloy of tin with lead or antimony. What is called Britannia-ware is a kind of pewter. When glass and earthen-ware were not as cheap as they are now, people very generally used to eat upon pewter platters and drink out of pewter mugs.

Brass, I have told you, is an alloy of copper and zinc. There are various other alloys of these metals. You have heard of pinchbeck watches. These are made in imitation of gold watches. The pinchbeck differs from brass only in having more zinc in it. It looks like gold; why, then, is it not just as good? Because it will not keep on looking so. Gold, you know, does not tarnish. The oxygen of the air can not get any hold upon it at all; but it can get hold of both the zinc and the copper that compose the pinchbeck.

There is another alloy of copper and zinc, called tombac, which [illegible] into very thin leaves, making a spurious or [illegible] When this is finely powdered it is the so-called [illegible]

[illegible] heard of late years a great deal about German silver [illegible] is no silver in this at all. It is an alloy of copper, [illegible] another metal called nickel. It is this latter metal that, [illegible] gives the alloy its likeness to silver. There is [illegible] silver, nickel, and copper, which is a very good substitute [illegible] silver, and is much used for ornamental purposes. The [illegible] these metals in it are, silver 30, nickel 25, and copper [illegible]

[illegible] an alloy which is sometimes made a source of amusement [illegible] spoons are manufactured from it, which will immediately [illegible] melt if they are introduced into hot tea. This alloy is [illegible] of bismuth, lead, and tin; the proportions, bismuth 8, [illegible] tin 3.

[illegible] and silver in common use are not pure, but are alloys. [illegible] both of money and of the articles for use and ornament [illegible] of these metals.

[illegible] silver coin of the United States we have a tenth part [illegible] The object of the copper is to make the coin hard, so [illegible] not readily wear out. Silver used for other purposes [illegible] have just this proportion of copper. If it have more, [illegible] white lustre of the silver will be lessened.

[illegible] softer than silver. In order to harden it sufficiently, [illegible] of the gold coin of this country is an alloy of copper and [illegible] The word *carat* is used in expressing the amount of [illegible] any alloy of it. This word means one twenty-fourth.

CHAPTER XVIII.

ACIDS.

I HAVE told you about the union of oxygen with metals forming oxyds. Now most of the acids in the world are formed by the union of oxygen with certain substances which are not metals, such as sulphur, phosphorus, etc. I will, therefore, now notice some of these substances, and the acids which oxygen forms with them.

I have already told you much about two of the substances with which oxygen forms acids. One is carbon, with which oxygen forms the gas called carbonic acid; the other is nitrogen, a gas, with which oxygen forms that powerful liquid acid, nitric acid, commonly called aqua fortis.

Sulphur is another substance with which oxygen unites to form an acid, called by the chemist sulphuric acid, the common name of it being oil of vitriol. We see sulphur ordinarily in two forms, roll brimstone and the flowers of sulphur. The flowers of sulphur are obtained by heating the sulphur so as to make it rise in vapor, the vapor being condensed so as to form fine powder. The roll brimstone is obtained by melting the sulphur and letting it run into moulds.

Sulphur is very abundant in nature. It is found as sulphur, and sometimes in beautiful yellow crystals, in the neighborhood of volcanoes; but it is most abundant in combination with other substances. You have seen, in the chapters on the metals, that it is united with many of them, forming sulphurets. Then the mineral called gypsum, or plaster of Paris, of which there is a great deal in the world, has sulphur in it. And, besides, there is some sulphur in all vegetables and animals. It is the sulphur in egg that blackens a silver spoon, forming a sulphuret of silver over its surface.

Sulphur and oxygen are mild substances, but, united together in certain proportions, they produce an acid of the most corrosive character. Neither sulphur nor oxygen, applied to your skin, hurts it; but the acid composed of them, if applied to it, would stain, and sting, and eat it.

If you burn phosphorus in oxygen or in air, which contains oxygen, the phosphorus unites with the oxygen and forms phosphoric acid. This you saw in Chapter III. So, also, if charcoal burns in oxygen or air, it unites with the oxygen and forms carbonic acid. But if you burn sulphur in oxygen or in air, it does not form sulphuric acid. The sulphur does not get its full supply of oxygen as the phosphorus and carbon do. It must have a full supply to form sulphuric acid, but it is only partly supplied. With this partial supply it forms a gas, which we call sulphurous acid gas. This is the gas that you smell when you burn a sulphur match.

In the phosphoric acid the phosphorus has got all the oxygen that it can be made to unite with. So, also, in the carbonic acid, the carbon has all the oxygen that it can have. But in the sulphurous acid gas the sulphur has united with only two thirds of the oxygen that it can be made to unite with, and that it must unite with to form sulphuric acid.

air is phosphor*ous* acid. When phosphorus is actually burned, phosphor*ic* acid is formed, as you have before learned. Observe the difference between sulphur and phosphorus in this respect. Phosphorus, on mere exposure to the air, makes phosphorous acid, but sulphur must be actually burned to make sulphurous acid, as noticed on page 117. There is more oxygen in phosphoric acid than in phosphorous acid, just as there is more in sulphuric than in sulphurous.

I will mention some of the experiments that can be tried with phosphorus.

To prepare for some of these, put a piece of phosphorus, of the size of a large pea, into a phial containing half an ounce (a table-spoonful) of ether. Cork the phial, and let it stand for some days, giving it a shake occasionally. Pour off the liquid into another phial. It is a solution of phosphorus, and is ready for use.

Drop some of this solution upon the hands, and rub them briskly together. The ether will fly off in vapor, leaving the phosphorus on the hands. If you do this in the evening, and make the room dark, your hands will be covered with light. The reason is, that the phosphorus unites with the oxygen of the air, producing combustion. If you rub your hands, the light will increase, because the fire is made to burn more briskly. But what is the reason that the hands are not burned in doing this? It is because there is so little of the phosphorus that there is very little heat produced.

Moisten a lump of sugar with the solution of phosphorus, and drop it into hot water. The heat of the water sends both the phosphorus up to the surface, and, when they get ... of the air sets fire to the phosphorus, and this ... ether, and off they go in a flame together.

... of the solution upon some fine blotting-paper. The ... and, after it is all gone, the phosphorus takes ... up the paper. If the blotting-paper be laid upon ..., the phosphorus and ether will burn together, just ... rose from the hot water.

Phosphorus can be made to burn under water. If a stream of oxygen be directed by the tube *a*, Fig. 40, upon a bit of phosphorus under hot water, in the glass *b*, it will burn brilliantly, the oxygen uniting with the phosphorus in the burning.

Phosphorus is so eager to unite with the oxygen in the air that a little friction produces heat enough to make it unite with it, and so quickly as to burn. ..., phosphorus is one of the ingredients of the sub... the ends of matches.

... is a very poisonous substance, and is often used ... rats and mice. The rat electuary, as it is called, ... with some phosphorus in it. One dram of phosphorus ... up with eight ounces of hot water and eight of flour.

... is that which we have in vinegar. It is spirits of ... oxydized. Oxygen is added to the alcohol as it ... sulphur to make sulphuric acid, or to phosphorus to ... acid. Vinegar is very commonly made from ... the air come to it. In this case the oxygen of ... with the alcohol in the cider, and forms acetic acid.

The amount of this acid in vinegar is very small. There are only from two to five gallons in a hundred of the vinegar. The rest is mostly water.

Tartaric acid is an acid that exists in many fruits, sometimes as acid, and sometimes united with potash, forming the substance which we call cream of tartar. This substance is in the juice of the grape, and gathers upon the inside of wine-casks from the wine.

There are various other acids in different fruits, as the citric in lemons, oranges, currants, etc., the malic in apples and other fruits, the oxalic in sorrel.

There is a very remarkable acid, which I have not yet noticed, commonly called muriatic acid. It is composed of hydrogen and a very singular gas called chlorine. This gas, which has a pale greenish-yellow color, is one of the ingredients of common salt, and I shall tell you particularly about it in another chapter. There is one thing which is very curious about these two gases, hydrogen and chlorine, when they are mixed together. If they be mixed in the dark, and be kept there, they have no disposition to unite; but bring the mixture into the light, and the union takes place, forming the muriatic acid. If a beam of sunlight be thrown by reflection from a looking-glass upon the glass jar containing the mixture, the union is so rapid as to cause a violent explosion. To prevent any accident from the broken glass, a wire screen must be put over the jar before the light is made to shine upon it.

The chemists call this acid hydrochloric acid. You can readily see the reason of the name; it comes from the two gases which

compose it. The hydrogen gives it the first part of its name, *hydro*, and the chlorine the latter part, *chloric*.

What is commonly called muriatic acid is a solution of the hydrochloric acid, which is a gas, in water. There is a little more in weight of the water than of the gas.

A mixture of this acid with nitric acid is called *aqua regia*, that is, royal water, because it is the only liquid that will dissolve gold, the king of metals. It is very curious that neither of these strong acids alone can affect the gold, but let them make the attack together, and this king submits at once. The gold, in dissolving, is changed into a compound. It is done in this way. The nitric acid makes the gas chlorine, that is in the muriatic acid with hydrogen, part company from the hydrogen. The chlorine thus set free, having a great liking for gold, unites with it, forming a chloride of this metal. We do not get, therefore, a real solution of gold, but a solution of this chloride. Common salt is a chloride of a metal, and I shall tell you about this and other chlorides in another chapter.

Another remarkable acid I will barely notice. It is commonly called prussic acid. It is a most deadly poison. A drop or two put upon the tongue of a dog will kill him instantly. This acid is composed of carbon, nitrogen, and hydrogen. It exists in very minute quantities in bitter almonds, peach blossoms, the kernels of some of the stone fruits, etc., giving to them a peculiar odor and flavor. A flavor is often given to articles of food by the use of bitter almonds, peach-pits, etc.; but the quantity of prussic acid thus used is so very minute that it does no harm.

I told you, in the first part of this chapter, that most of the acids have oxygen in them; but prussic acid and hydrochloric acid have not. They have hydrogen instead, and so they are called hydrogen acids. There are not many of this class of acids compared with the oxygen acids.

Questions.—How are most of the acids formed? What two acids have you already learned considerable about? State some things in regard to them. What acid does sulphur form with oxygen? Describe the two forms in which we have sulphur. What is said of the abundance of sulphur? What of its combination with other substances? Why does egg blacken the spoon with which you eat it? What is said of the difference between sulphuric acid and the ingredients that compose it? How do carbon and phosphorus differ from sulphur in uniting with oxygen? How does sulphurous acid gas differ from phosphoric acid and carbonic acid? Tell how sulphuric acid is made. What would happen if sulphuric acid were formed whenever sulphur is burned? What is said of the affinity of sulphuric acid for water? What effect does this union produce? Describe the experiment represented in Fig. 39. Give the other experiment. From what is phosphorus commonly obtained? Describe phosphorus. What care should be exercised in experimenting with it? Tell about the solution of phosphorus in ether. Tell what the effect is when some is put upon the face and hands, and explain it. Give the experiment with sugar. Give that with blotting-paper. Explain Fig. 40. What is acetic acid? Explain the chemistry of making vinegar. How much acetic acid is there in vinegar? What is said of tartaric acid? Mention some of the acids found in plants. Of what is muriatic acid composed? Describe the influence of light upon the union of chlorine and hydrogen. Explain the name *hydrochloric* given to muriatic acid. What is really the liquid commonly called muriatic acid? What is said of *aqua regia?* What of prussic acid? What are hydrogen acids?

CHAPTER XIX.

SALTS.

I HAVE told you about oxyds, which are formed by the union of oxygen with the metals. I have also told you about the acids, which are, most of them, formed by the union of oxygen with certain substances, as sulphur, phosphorus, carbon, nitrogen, etc. Now these acids unite with these oxyds to form what are called salts.

The term salt is applied by the chemist to any substance composed of an acid and an oxyd. Thus nitric acid united with potash forms the salt called by the chemist nitrate of potash, and by people generally saltpetre. So sulphuric acid united with potash forms the salt called sulphate of potash. It may seem odd to you to speak of chalk as a salt, but it is so called by the chemist because it is composed of an acid, carbonic acid, and an oxyd, lime, together forming the carbonate of lime.

Observe that the acids do not unite with the metals, but with the oxyds of the metals. Thus nitric acid does not unite with potassium, but with the oxyd of this metal, potash. It is so with all metals and all acids. In forming a salt a compound unites with a compound. The oxyd is a compound of oxygen and a metal, and the acid is a compound of oxygen and some substance, as sulphur. So it seems that there must be oxygen on both sides, or the acid will not unite.

Observe the names of the salts. You can always tell by the

name which the chemist gives to a salt of what it is composed. Thus, take nitrate of potash. The termination of the first word in the name is *ate*, and signifies that the substance is a salt, and the first part of the word shows what acid is in the salt. Then potash is the name of the oxyd, the other part of the salt. So, also, the acid in sulphate of potash is sulphuric acid, and that in carbonate of potash is carbonic acid.

But there are some salts the names of which have the termination of the first word in *ite* instead of *ate*. These salts are formed with acids whose names end in *ous*, while the salts which have *ate* in their names are formed with acids whose names end in *ic*. Thus sulphite of soda has sulphurous acid in it, while sulphate of soda has in it sulphuric acid. The salts whose names end in *ate* are much more common than those whose names end in *ite*. The former have more oxygen in them than the latter, for the acids that have their names end in *ic* have more oxygen than those whose names end in *ous*.

Some of the metals have no special names for their oxyds, as potassium, sodium, etc., have. In such cases the name of the metal is used in giving the name of the salts. Thus we say carbonate of iron. It would be more correct to say carbonate of the oxyd of iron. This would be too long, and so we leave out a part of the name. If this oxyd had any short name, as the oxyd of potassium has, we should use it.

An acid and an oxyd are very different from each other. This is especially true of the alkalies. They have qualities just opposite to those of the acids. The taste of potash, for instance, is the very opposite of sour; and all its other qualities, as you will learn in my next book on Chemistry, are the opposite of those of an acid. But when an acid and an alkali unite together in certain proportions, the acid destroys all the alkaline qualities of the alkali, and the alkali destroys all the acid properties of the acid.

The white powder which you know by the common name of cream of tartar is a salt composed of tartaric acid and potash. But this is sour, as you know, if you have ever taken it as a medicine. How is this? Why is it that in this case the acid properties are not destroyed by the alkali? It is because there is not enough of the alkali united with the acid to do it. The salt is not as sour as the tartaric acid itself, for a part of the acid quality is destroyed by the potash.

There is another salt, made of the same ingredients, in which there is enough potash to destroy all the acid properties of the acid. It is called tartrate of potash, while the cream of tartar is called the *super*tartrate of potash. Cream of tartar has this name because there is more tartaric acid in it than there is in the tartrate of potash. It is for the same reason that a thing is called superfine when it is more than fine, or superexcellent when it is more than excellent.

Cream of tartar is sometimes called, also, the bitartrate of potash. This is because the Latin word *bis* means twice, for this salt has exactly twice as much tartaric acid in it as the tartrate of potash has. So there is a carbonate of soda and a bicarbonate of soda. There is just twice as much carbonic acid in the bicarbonate as in the carbonate.

A salt in which there is just enough of alkali to destroy the

Carbonate of lime does not readily dissolve in water. But water will dissolve some, especially if there be carbonic acid gas in the water. The water that comes from some springs has, for this reason, considerable of this salt in it, and some of it stops upon stones and sticks above the spring, crusting them over. In some caves in limestone regions we have beautiful displays of the formation of limestone from water in which this salt is dissolved. As the water drips from any spot in the roof of the cave, some of the carbonate of lime stays upon the roof. Then, as more and more adheres, there forms a projection pointing downward, very much like an icicle as water drips in cold weather from the eaves of a house. At the same time, there is formed underneath, on the floor of the cave, a little hillock of the limestone from the water that drops there. That which forms above is called a stalactite, and that below a stalagmite.

Fig. 41.

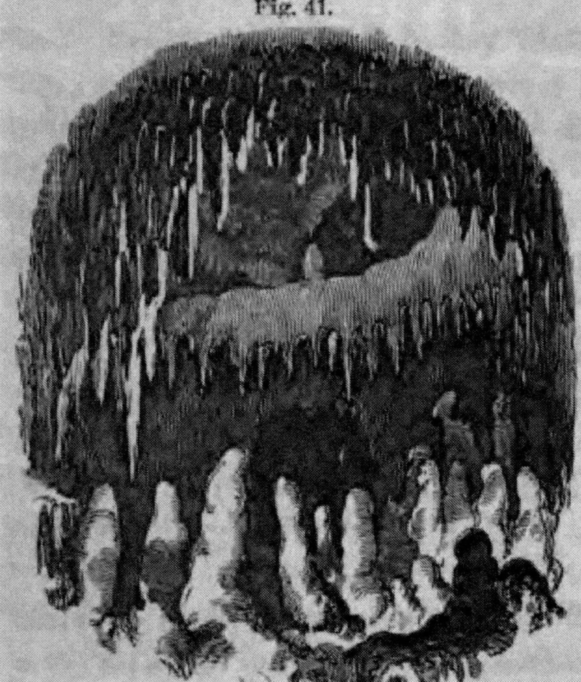

Sometimes, when there are many of these stalactites and stalagmites, and they have been forming for a long time so as to reach a great size, they make a splendid appearance. In Fig. 41 you have a picture of the Hall of Statuary, as it is called, in Weyer's Cave in Virginia.

[illegible] and stalagmites present every variety of form [illegible] lighted up with torches, the place looks like [illegible]ment.

[illegible] something about quick-lime on page 97. This [illegible] there, the oxyd of calcium. It is commonly [illegible] carbonate of lime. The limestone or the chalk is [illegible] heat in the flame of a furnace. This makes [illegible] acid quit the lime and fly off into the air. Lime, [illegible] oxyd of calcium, is left behind.

[illegible] of potash is a very different substance from carbonate [illegible] likes water very much, and dissolves in it readily. [illegible] plants, and therefore is obtained from ashes. Not [illegible] ago it was common for every family in the country [illegible] was called a leach-tub. In this were put the ashes. [illegible] kept wet, there was always a running out, from a [illegible] a liquid called ley. This contained the carbonate [illegible] caustic potash together in solution. There is caus[illegible] well as the carbonate, because there is lime in ashes. [illegible] is this: Lime, having a greater affinity for car[illegible] than potash has, takes away this gas from some of the [illegible] thus changing it into potash. The quantity of the [illegible] potash in the ley is increased by putting some lime into [illegible] of the leach-tub. The effect of this is to change much [illegible] carbonate of potash into caustic potash than would [illegible] by the little lime that is in the ashes. Leach-tubs are [illegible] out of use in families, as potash is made from [illegible] in large establishments.

[illegible] of carbonate of potash and caustic potash is call[illegible]

ed simply potash by people generally, but this is not strictly correct, for this name belongs properly only to caustic potash, that is, the oxyd of potassium.

I have told you that if carbonate of lime be heated strongly, the carbonic acid is driven off. Carbonate of potash is very different in this respect. The hottest fire can not drive off the carbonic acid from it. If heat could do it we should not have any carbonate of potash in ashes, but caustic potash, the carbonic acid having been carried off by the burning into the air.

Here is a little experiment that you can try with carbonate of potash. Drop a teaspoonful of this salt into a tumbler half full of vinegar. There will be a brisk effervescence, a gas escaping from the liquid. Lower, now, a burning taper into the tumbler, as represented in Fig. 42. It will go out. Why? Because the gas which comes up and fills the tumbler is carbonic acid. The acetic acid in the vinegar takes the potash away from the carbonic acid, because it has a greater affinity for it. A salt is formed in this experiment by the union of the acetic acid and the potash. You can tell what the name of it is by observing what I have told you about the names of salts on page 126.

Fig. 42.

If you dissolve some potash in water, and then boil in the solution some dirty greasy rags, the solution will become very dark and dirty, but the rags will be white and clean. There is chemistry in this. The potash has an affinity for the grease, and in the water we have the two united together; but in getting together, the dirt has been taken out of the cloth with the grease by the potash. This explains the use of soap in washing. In making common soft soap the potash is united with grease or fat and water, but there is not so much grease as to prevent the potash from uniting with more grease. The potash alone would be a very harsh material to wash with, but by mixing it with grease and water we make a very smooth article that we can use easily. In washing clothes the potash in it takes out all the oily matter which has come from the perspiration, and with it the dirt: and if there be dirt alone without any oily matter, the soap readily mingles with it, so that the water can take it out better than it can without the soap.

Here is some poetry which some one has written about soap:

"Some water and oil
One day had a broil,
As down in a glass they were dropping,
And would not unite,
But continued to fight,
Without any prospect of stopping.

Some pearlash o'erheard—
As quick as a word,
He jumped in the midst of the clashing;
When all three agreed,
And united with speed,
And *soap* was created for washing."

I must find a little fault with this poetry, pretty and amusing as it is. The water and oil do not have any "broil" when we try to mix them together. They simply will not have any thing to do with each other. As soon as you stop shaking them in a ves-

iron better than it does copper, that which is close by the iron quits the copper to take the iron. It unites with the iron and forms sulphate of iron. This salt, as it forms, is dissolved in the water, and the copper clings to the iron, giving it the red color.

This experiment explains the manner in which the metal copper is sometimes obtained in some mines from a solution of this salt. At one time, in Wicklow, Ireland, five hundred tons of iron bars were placed in pits that were full of this solution of sulphate of copper. In about a year the bars were all gone. What had become of them? The sulphuric acid in the sulphate of copper had quit the copper and united with the iron to form sulphate of iron. The copper lay at the bottom of the pits, in a sort of reddish mud. This was taken out, and the copper freed from what was mixed with it, and, by melting, was put into proper shape for use.

Alum is a sulphate, but it is not a sulphate of *one* oxyd, as the sulphates are that I have mentioned. It is a sulphate of two oxyds; it has two strings to its bow, as we may say. It is sulphuric acid united with potash and alumina. Potash I have said so much about that you are well acquainted with it. Alumina I have noticed on page 108. Alum is a *double salt*, as it is termed. There are many of such salts. The medicine called tartar emetic is a double salt. It is a tartrate of potash and antimony.

Nitrate of potash, formed by the union of nitric acid and potash, is commonly called either nitre or saltpetre. It is chiefly interesting as being one of the ingredients of gunpowder. This article is made of three things, nitre, charcoal, and sulphur. They are very carefully mixed. When fire is touched to this mixture

it readily burns, and in the burning a great quantity of gas i produced all at once. It is this gas, striving to get room for i self, that drives the ball out of the gun or cannon, as is fully ex plained in the chapter on Powder in the Third Part of the Child' Book of Nature.

But how is this gas produced? Let us look at this. The nitr is composed of nitric acid and potash. Now there is oxygen ga in both nitric acid and potash, and this oxygen quickly unite with the carbon or charcoal, forming a great amount of carboni acid gas. In doing this it sets free the nitrogen gas which wa with it in the nitric acid, this acid being composed, as you learne in Chapter III., of oxygen and nitrogen. Carbonic acid gas an nitrogen are then the chief gases that are set free in firing gun powder, and produce the explosion.

Think how great the change is in this case. From a sma quantity of powder comes out, all at once, a very large bulk o gases. I say comes out, for the gases were in that powder locke up, and squeezed, as we may say, into small quarters. And se what it is that sets free these condensed gases. It is our livel friend oxygen, waked up by fire to assert its affinities.

I will notice only one other nitrate, the nitrate of silver. Th is a white caustic salt. It is used in making indelible ink. It used also in the mixtures for coloring the hair dark.

The acetate of lead is commonly called sugar of lead, becaus it has a sweet taste. It seems strange that it should have such taste when one of its ingredients is so sharp an acid. You ca have some idea of its sharpness when you call to mind that makes but about the twentieth part of the sharpest vinegar.

I will describe a beautiful experiment that you can try with this salt. Dissolve half an ounce of sugar of lead in six ounces (twelve tablespoonsful) of water, in a phial. Fasten in the cork a rod or stick of zinc, as you see in Fig. 43. You will soon see a change taking place. The zinc will begin to have little spangles upon it, and these will gradually branch out in all directions, forming a sort of tree. This tree is made of the metal lead, and is called the lead tree.* The explanation is this. The acetic acid has a stronger affinity for zinc than it has for lead. It therefore leaves the lead and unites with the zinc to form acetate of zinc. The lead, which is separated from the acid, forms the tree, while the acetate of zinc dissolves in the water, taking the place there of the acetate of lead. It takes a day or two for the tree to be completed. If, on making the solution in the phial, it is not perfectly clear, you can make it so by adding a little good vinegar.

Fig. 43.

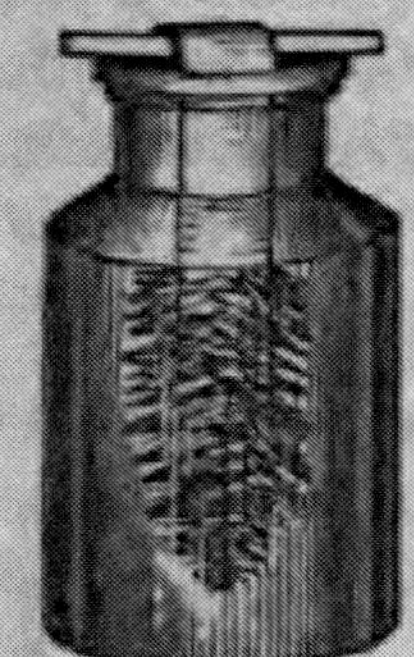

The change of the acid in this experiment from the lead over to the zinc is like the change of sulphuric acid from the copper to the iron in the experiment with sulphate of copper given on page 139. In both cases the acid quits one metal to unite with another which it likes better.

* This tree can be made to have different shapes by a little contrivance. Fasten a small lump of zinc to the under side of the cork by a string through the cork. Then fasten to the zinc some fine brass or copper wire, which you can make branch out in various directions. The crystals of lead will collect on these branches, and this will give a more perfect tree shape than the slip of zinc will.

I will notice but one other acetate, that of copper, commonly called verdigris. This is a green-colored salt, and is very poisonous. It is used in painting. Whenever acetic acid comes in contact with copper, this salt is formed. You can see, therefore, how dangerous it would be to have any cooking operation in which vinegar is used done in a copper vessel.

Questions.—What are the chemical name and composition of gypsum? Why is it called plaster of Paris? What is said of the difference between gypsum and its ingredients? What of the difference between lime and sulphuric acid and their ingredients? What is alabaster, and for what is it used? What is satin spar? What is meant by *foliated* gypsum? Explain how gypsum is used in making casts. How can you copy coins with powdered gypsum? What is said of hard finish? What are the chemical name and composition of Glauber's salt? What are Epsom salts? Why are these two salts called neutral salts? Give the chemical name and composition of the three vitriols. State the knife-blade experiment. State and explain the facts in regard to the copper-mine in Ireland. What are the chemical name and composition of alum? What are double salts? Give the chemical name and composition of tartar emetic. What is the composition of saltpetre? Of what is gunpowder composed? How does it exert such force when fired? What are the gases set free in discharging it, and how are they produced? What is said of the change produced in the powder? What is said of the nitrate of silver? What of the acetate of lead? Describe and explain the formation of the lead tree. How is the change here like that in the copper-mine related on page 140? What is said of the acetate of copper?

CHAPTER XXII.

SHELLS, CORALS, AND BONES.

THE shells that you pick up on the sea-shore are made of carbonate of lime. All oyster-shells are made of this substance. The lime which is used for making mortar and other purposes is often obtained from oyster-shells, just as we obtain it from limestone. It is obtained by burning them; that is, by heating them very strongly. The heat, as you have before learned, drives off the carbonic acid gas, and leaves the lime alone.

From whence comes all this carbonate of lime of which the shells are made? It is in the water, dissolved in it as the salt is. But how does it get into the water? It comes from the earth and the rocks of limestone. It is washed along with the water as it runs in brooks and rivers, and at length comes to the sea. Here there is more of it in the water than any where else.

But how, think you, is this carbonate of lime made into shells? Does it gather from the water on the outside of the animals that live in them? Does the oyster, for example, just lie still, and let the shell grow on him by having the carbonate of lime settle upon him by little and little from the water, as it crusts upon a stone or a stick in a spring? No, this is not the way. All that big rough shell has been swallowed by the oyster, and has been in his blood. Only a little at a time was swallowed, dissolved in the sea-water; but that little was used in building his shell-house to cover him.

Look at an oyster's shell carefully. There are different layers. The outside layer is smaller than the next one, and this is smaller than the next, and so on; and the one next to the oyster is the largest. The outside layer was made when the oyster was very small—a baby oyster, as we may say. Then, as he grew a little larger, another layer was formed from the carbonate of lime as it oozed out from his skin, and so on to the last and largest.

All shells are not made exactly after the plan of the oyster-shell; but it is as true of them all as it is of the oyster-shell, that every particle of them has been swallowed in the water drank by the animals that lived in them.

There is one class of animals that live in the sea which make a singular use of the carbonate of lime that they continually swallow. I mean the coral animals, as they are called. These little animals always stay exactly where they are born. They are fixed to a strong foundation. That foundation is their skeleton, formed from the carbonate of lime which they have swallowed. This skeleton extends up into the animal's body. The animal is all the time growing upward in the water, and adds continually to the top of its skeleton. In the mean time the lower part of its body is always dying. It dies below while it grows above.

You see what the effect of all this is. The animal is building a column of carbonate of lime, he being all the time at the top of it, sitting on it like a well-fitted cap.

But these animals always live in companies and build together. If a great many of them, then, build together their columns alongside of each other, there will be a great deal of building done, though each does but little.

You will be surprised when I tell you that whole islands have been built in this way. Long ranges of coast, sometimes for hundreds of miles, have been lined with reefs built up by these little animals. Some of the tiny builders that do such work are no larger than the head of a pin.

These little reef-builders have done a vast deal of work in one part of our country—in Florida; and they are engaged in the same work now. Once there was no Florida. The peninsula we call by this name was not there. The sea covered what is now dry land. This was centuries upon centuries ago. Florida, since that, has been built up, and the work has been done by the little coral animals. All the foundation of Florida has been gathered from the water by them. Yes, it had to be actually swallowed by animals before it could be made into Florida.

I will show you a little how this building was done. All along the coast of Florida, a little way out from the main land, there are islands called keys. These have been built up by the coral animals. They began their work down deep at the bottom of the sea, and worked along upward till they reached the surface. Then their work was done, for they can not work out of water; and their work being done, they died.

But something more needs to be done to make these coral reefs fit to live upon, for they are merely plains, as we may call them, of carbonate of lime, which just come to the surface of the water, and when it is high water they are entirely covered. After a while they do become real islands, and things grow upon them, and people live there. I will tell you how this is done. The waves, dashing over the reefs, break them up somewhat, and the pieces are washed up toward the middle of the reef. At the same time, the dirty stuff of various kinds washed about in the sea collects there also, and the sea-weed is thrown up upon the heaps in considerable quantities by the waves. All this gradually forms a soil upon the reef, and makes it a real island. Seeds are dropped there by birds, or are carried there in the water, and are washed up on to the land. Grass, flowers, shrubs, and trees soon grow there, and then man comes and plants such things as he wishes to have grow, and builds his habitation.

These islands along the coast of Florida will, after a while, join to the main land; that is, become a part of Florida itself. How is this? The space between the main land and the islands is continually filling up with mud, which washes in there, and after a long time there will be so much of it as to make dry land. All Florida has been made in this way. Island after island has been built up by the coral animals, covered with soil, and then joined to the main land in the way that I have pointed out.

But you will ask why the coral-builders do their work away from the main land, instead of building up upon the edge of the shore. This is because the work is begun by coral animals that are fond of deep water, and can not live in shallow water. They work away, swallowing stone and laying it down, till they come up somewhere near the surface of the water. Their work is now done, and they die. Then another set of coral-builders, that are fitted to live in shallow water, go to building on the foundations laid by their deep-water friends.

Different kinds of coral animals have different fashions in building. There are beautiful specimens of their various work to be

CHAPTER XXIII.

GLASS AND EARTHENWARE.

You will think it strange when I tell you that, in treating the subjects named at the head of this chapter, I shall introduce you to a certain class of *salts*. Yet, surprising to you as it is, in glass and earthenware we have salts made with an acid, like the other salts of which I have told you.

The acid which is in these salts is of a very peculiar character. Most acids, you know, are decidedly sour to the taste, and are liquid, as sulphuric acid, nitric acid, acetic acid, etc. There is, indeed, one acid that I have told you much about, carbonic acid, which is a gas, and has rather a pleasant, lively, but scarcely acid taste, as you perceive in drinking soda-water. But the acid which we have in glass and earthenware is much more singular than this. It has no taste, and is solid, very solid. It is the substance which you see in flint, and in quartz or rock crystal, as it is called. The shining, clear grains which you see in sand are composed of this acid. It is called silicic acid, or silica. The latter is the name most often given to it. Very hard substances are these grains in the sand, and, if you put them into your mouth, so far from being sour, they are entirely tasteless.

Why, then, is this silica considered an acid? For several reasons, which I will now give you.

One reason is, that, like most of the acids which I have mentioned, it is composed of oxygen united with another substance.

[illegible] sulphuric acid is composed of oxygen and sulphur, and [illegible] acid of oxygen and carbon, so silicic acid, or silica, is [illegible] of oxygen and a substance called silicon.

[illegible] reason is, that silica acts like the acids in regard to [illegible] substances. Thus, as sulphuric acid unites with lime, form[illegible] sulphate of lime, and carbonic acid unites with it to form car[illegible] of lime, so silica, or silicic acid, unites with lime to form a [illegible] which we call silicate of lime.

[illegible] perhaps you will ask, why not consider this silica an oxyd [illegible] of an acid—an oxyd of silicon—as it is composed of sili[illegible] oxygen? First, because nearly all oxyds are formed [illegible], and silicon does not appear at all like a metal. Then, [illegible] silica were an oxyd, it should unite with acids to form [illegible] the oxyds do; but this it can not in any way be made to [illegible] On the other hand, it unites with oxyds, as is the case with [illegible] acids.

[illegible] is a very important part of some plants. It is in the [illegible] of all grass, giving them such firmness that they can stand [illegible] It is also in the stalks of all grain. It is to these and some [illegible] plants very much what bones are to animals. In some [illegible] there is so much of silica that they are used for scouring.

[illegible] how does this flint or silica get into plants? If you even [illegible] it very fine indeed, and put it into water, none of it will [illegible]. It seems strange, then, that any of it should go with [illegible] up into any plant. To do this, it must be made very fine, [illegible] finer than we can make it by pounding and grinding; and [illegible] done in some way, we know not how, about the roots of [illegible]. But this is not enough; it must be changed so as to make

of alumina. But all clay, as we find it, contains more or less of other silicates, of lime, of potash, etc.

The brownish-red color of bricks and common flower-pots is owing to the rust of iron which is in the clay.

Bricks, you know, are quite porous, and so water will soak into them. This is also the case with common flower-pots. This porousness will do us no harm in this case, but generally it is necessary to have earthenware so made that no fluid can escape through its pores. It would not answer, for example, to keep preserves in jars of porous earthenware. The watery part would gradually escape through the pores, and the preserves would become dry.

The difficulty is remedied in two ways. One is to glaze the surface of the earthenware; that is, a glass surface is made. This is done in various ways. One method you will be interested in, because you can understand the chemistry of it. The fumes of common salt are made to go up all about the articles of earthenware when they are very hot. Now salt is composed of the gas chlorine and the metal sodium. I told you a little about chlorine on page 122, and I shall tell you more particularly about it in the next chapter. You learned something about sodium in Chapter XIV. In the glazing the chlorine leaves the sodium to unite with some of the iron in the earthenware. Then the sodium, thus left by the chlorine, becomes soda by taking some oxygen; and this soda unites with the silica in the earthenware to form a silicate of soda, thus making a soda glass, as we may call it. So you have a coating of this glass all over the articles.

Another mode of making earthenware impervious to water

is to make the ware partly earthen and partly glass. The ingredients are so selected that you may have the silicates of lime, potash, etc., of which glass is made, thoroughly united with the silicate of alumina or clay. This stops up all the pores, and does not merely shut those which are outside, as the glazing does.

Questions.—To what class of substances in chemistry do glass and earthenware belong? What are the qualities of most acids? How does carbonic acid differ from them? What is silica? In what substances do you see it? How is it unlike other acids? What is the first reason given for calling it an acid? What is the second reason? Why do we not call silica an oxyd? What is said about its being present in plants? How does it get into them? What is said about its being deposited in the right place? Tell about silica in mortar. What are the salts made by silica called? What is common window-glass? Tell how it is made, and explain the chemistry of the process. What is said of soluble glass? How are the various colors of glass produced? Relate the anecdote about the discovery of the way to make glass. What truth does this illustrate? What is in earthenware? How is it in porcelain, in flower-pots, in bricks? What is the composition of pure clay? What else is there commonly with it? What is the cause of the brownish-red color of flower-pots and bricks? What is said about their porousness? What is glazing, and what is the use of it? Describe and explain glazing with salt. Describe another way of making earthenware impervious to water.

CHAPTER XXIV.

CHLORINE, BLEACHING, AND COMMON SALT.

THE salts which I have noticed in the previous chapters are made with acids; but there are some salts in which there is no acid. They are formed by the union of certain simple substances with a metal. Common salt is one of these salts. In this substance we have, as stated in the previous chapter, the metal sodium united with a very singular gas called chlorine, and so the chemists call it the chloride of sodium.

You remember that all the compounds of the gas oxygen formed with metals are called oxyds, or oxides, as it is sometimes spelt; so all the compounds of this gas chlorine are called chlorides. Salt is a chloride of sodium, as soda is an oxyd of it.

Before I tell you particularly about salt I will speak of the gas chlorine. It is one of the gases that has color. Its color is a greenish-yellow. It has a powerful and very peculiar odor, It is very injurious if breathed in any quantity. Even when diluted with considerable air it is very suffocating. If you should breathe it without any air mixed with it you would die. Yet to breathe a very little of it, mixed with a great deal of air, does no harm, and it is supposed by some physicians that it is beneficial to those who have consumption.

Chlorine is of great use in purifying foul air. You perhaps have seen chloride of lime, moistened, set round in dishes where

of such a kind as to cause bad odors. It is the comes from this that purifies the air. The little that escapes into the air in this case, although you smell strongly, does no harm to your breathing, for it is very diluted with air.

odor of this gas is so peculiar that if you have ever smelled you always know it afterward. You smell it wherever bleaching of cloth going on. You smell it, therefore, mills, for the rags out of which the paper is made are by it.

tell you about this bleaching. If you put a rag of calico of chlorine gas, no effect will be produced on its colors; moisten the rag before it is put in, and the colors will be out by the chlorine at once. Chlorine must have water it will not bleach.

gas will dissolve in water, and the solution is very to use in bleaching. A calico rag dipped in it is very made white. It will take out ink-spots also. It has no ef- printers' ink, however, nor can it bleach woolens.

the great usefulness of chlorine in making paper. paper can be made out of rags of all colors, because the be removed by the chlorine. You see, too, its useful- whitening cloth. The old method of doing this was very was to spread cloth out upon grass for the sun, and rain, to whiten. This, called *grass-bleaching*, took weeks; but, *bleaching* by chlorine, we can do the same thing in Some care is required not to have the chlorine and to get all the chlorine out of the cloth after

the bleaching is done. If this care is not exercised the c lose some of its strength, some of the substance of the cl eaten out as well as the coloring matter.

Exactly how chlorine bleaches you are not sufficie vanced in chemistry to understand, and that I shall expl next book.

You can make chlorine in this way. Pour into a pi two tablespoonsful of common sulphuric acid, and ad more than the same quantity of chloride of lime, or b powder. Add the powder gradually, covering the bott slip of glass each time after dropping some i resented in Fig. 44. Chlorine made in this answer for many of the experiments.

Fig. 44.

The explanation is this: The sulphuric a ing a stronger affinity for lime than chlo takes the lime and unites with it. The chl ing thus separated from the lime, rises up the bottle.

Another method is to put some black oxyd of manga a flask, and pour in enough muriatic acid to cover the seen in Fig. 45. Gentle heat must be applied, and the pass over into the bottle which is placed t it. You observe that the tube reaches to tom of the bottle. This is to have the chl push up the air which is in the bottle, readily does, taking its place in the bottl two and a half times as heavy as air, and so has no dispo escape upward. You can tell when the bottle is full by t

Fig. 45.

When it is full slip it out from under the tube, cork it, and place the tube in another bottle.

The explanation of the formation of chlorine in this way is easy. The oxyd of manganese has a great deal of oxygen in it, while the muriatic acid is composed of hydrogen and chlorine, as you learned on page 122. The hydrogen of the acid unites with the oxygen of the oxyd of manganese, so that the chlorine of the acid is set at liberty.

Fig. 46.

Although chlorine gas is so destructive to life when breathed, it supports combustion. If a taper, Fig. 46, be introduced into a bottle of this gas, it burns with a dull red flame, and a thick cloud of smoke. The explanation is this: Chlorine has a strong affinity for hydrogen, but none for carbon. It therefore unites with the hydrogen of the taper or candle, and the flame, heating the carbon that is with the hydrogen in the taper, sends it upward in a dense smoke.

Fig. 47.

So, also, if a slip of paper, moistened with oil of turpentine, be introduced into a bottle of chlorine, Fig. 47, the hydrogen of the turpentine will burn, while its carbon will pass off unburnt in smoke.

See how very widely both of the ingredients of salt differ from the compound which they make. Chlorine is a gas of most powerful odor, very suffocating, so that to breathe it clear is to die. Sodium is a metal which, if put on your tongue, would take fire, and turn into a caustic. Yet this gas and metal together form a very mild, pleasant salt, which is a part of the food of man and beast every where.

CHAPTER XXV.

CHLORIDES, IODIDES, BROMIDES, AND SEA-WATER.

I HAVE, in the previous chapter, told you about one chloride, the chloride of sodium. But there are many other chlorides, for chlorine unites with many of the metals. With some it unites with such eagerness that they burn together. Thus, if you sprinkle a fine powder of the metal antimony into a jar of chlorine gas, each particle will take fire. You will therefore have a shower of fire in the jar, and there will be a white smoke. This smoke is composed of very small particles of chloride of antimony; for in the burning the chlorine and antimony unite together.

There are two chlorides of mercury, which are very different from each other. One is calomel, and the other is corrosive sublimate. The difference in their composition is that the corrosive sublimate has exactly twice as much chlorine in it as the calomel. The calomel is called, therefore, the chloride of mercury, while the corrosive sublimate is the bichloride. This difference in the proportion of chlorine makes a vast difference in the qualities of the two substances. The corrosive sublimate is very soluble in water, but the calomel will not dissolve at all. The corrosive sublimate is a violent eating or corrosive poison, as its name indicates. If it be swallowed it burns the stomach and all of the passage to it. But the calomel is a white powder, like flour, that produces no irritation when taken into the mouth.

Some families keep a bottle of corrosive sublimate, dissolved in some liquor, as bed-bug poison, for it will kill this and other bugs when put upon them. Sometimes, from carelessness, this poison has been drank, and many deaths have been caused in this way. Now every body ought to know exactly what to do when this accident happens, for what is to be done must be done quickly. The individual must be made to swallow very freely of the whites of eggs. This is the best thing; but, if there be no eggs at hand, milk or flour stirred up in water can be used.

While chlorine makes with sodium so mild a salt, it forms with zinc a very caustic one. The chloride of zinc is used as a caustic considerably by surgeons.

There are many other chlorides, but it would not be interesting to you to hear about them.

There is a great deal of chlorine in the world, but the most of it is in the salt-water of the sea, combined with sodium.

There is another substance, similar to chlorine in many respects, in sea-water and in sea-plants. It is called iodine. It exists in sea-water combined with the metals sodium and potassium, as chlorine is combined with sodium. In some sea-plants there is considerable of it, and it is from a ley made with the ashes of such plants that it is obtained.

Fig. 48.

Iodine is a solid substance, looking something like black-lead, but darker in color. If heated it turns into a splendid purple vapor or gas, which is one of the heaviest of the gases. If you put a few grains of it in a jar, *a*, Fig. 48, and place the jar in a sand-bath,* *b*, warmed

* A sand-bath is simply fine sand in a dish. The object is to apply the heat gradually. This can be done, however, with a spirit-lamp alone, by keeping it at a little distance from the glass jar.

Most of the solid matter that is dissolved in sea-water is common salt. Next to this in quantity are the compounds of magnesium—the chloride of magnesium and the sulphate and carbonate of magnesia. It is these that give the bitter taste, especially the sulphate of magnesia or Epsom salts. If you have ever taken any of this as a medicine you will recognize the resemblance between its taste and the bitter taste of sea-water.

There is a comparatively small amount of these saline matters in rivers, because the water in them is always moving on to empty into lakes and seas. There is little commonly in lakes, because the water is running out of them as constantly as it runs in. Thus the water that runs into our great chain of lakes in the north runs out through the River St. Lawrence into the Atlantic ocean.

There are some inland seas and lakes that contain more saline matters than the ocean itself. This is partly because they have no outlet, and are alone by themselves, and partly because there is much salt in the neighborhood. The Caspian Sea, the Dead Sea, and Lake Aral are of this kind.

All the saline matters in the water of rivers, and lakes, and seas, were once in the rocks of the earth, and were carried off by the water which is every where so busy. But, for the most part, before this was done, they were in various ways broken off from the rocks and ground up, so as to make a part of the earth under our feet. Here the water found them, and carried them off into the brooks, and rivers, and seas.

But much of all this is returned, in various ways, from the water to the earth again. I will give but one example of this.

ral animals, that I told you about in Chapter XXII., tak- carbonate of lime which the earth has supplied to the give it back to the earth in reefs, and islands, and penin-

more salt there is in water the heavier it is, and the more bear up solid substances. Thus a man floating in common only has a part of his head above the surface, but in the of the Dead Sea it costs him no effort to keep breast high A ship there would easily carry a load which would sink water almost any where else.

Fig. 50.

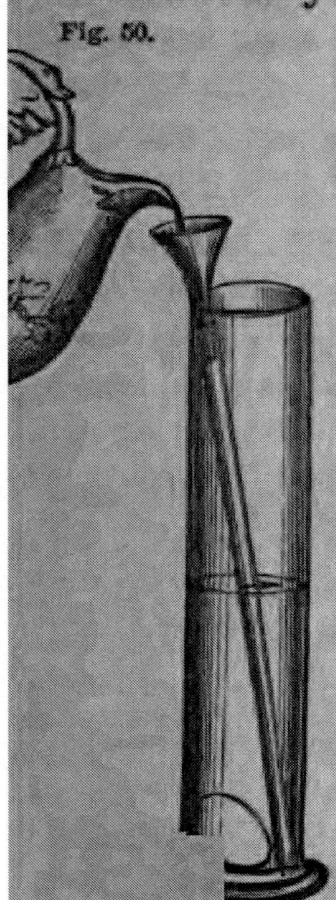

There are some pretty experiments which show the difference between salt and fresh water in regard to floating substances. Suppose that you have an egg in a jar half full of water. The egg will be at the bottom of the jar, for it is heavier than water. Pour now some strong brine into the bottom of the jar through a long tube, as represented in Fig. 50. The brine will force up the lighter water, and with it the egg. The egg will remain at the middle part of the jar, at the bottom of the fresh water, floating on the brine, just as a piece of wood would float on the surface of water in the jar, at the bottom of the air, if the jar were half full of water, air of course being above it.

Experiment.

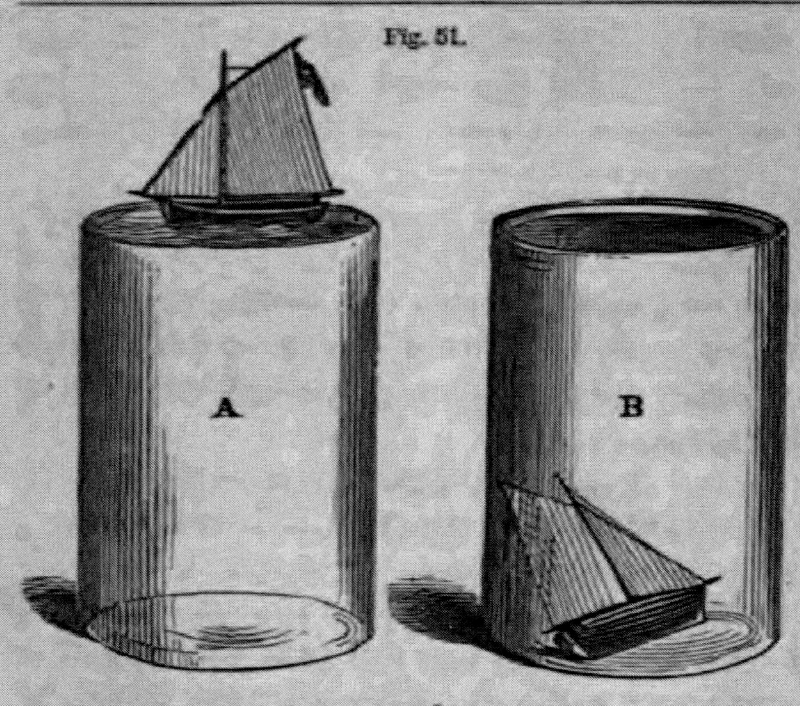

Fig. 51.

A very pretty experiment is represented in Fig. 51. The jar A is filled with brine. A little toy ship is floating upon it. To have the experiment succeed, the ship must be so loaded that it will just float upon the brine. If now you place the ship in the jar of fresh water, B, it will sink.

Questions.—What substances are formed by the union of chlorine with metals? What is remarked about this union in some cases? What is said about the two chlorides of mercury? What about poisoning with corrosive sublimate, and the antidote? What is said of the chloride of zinc? Where is most of the chlorine that is in the world? Where is iodine found, and in combination with what? Describe this substance. Explain Fig. 48. State what is represented in Fig. 49, and explain it. What are iodides, and what is said of some of them? Describe bromine. What is said of the quantity of it in sea-water? With what is it united? What is said of its poisonous character? To what use has it been applied? What is said of the three substances peculiar to sea-water? What are the solid substances that sea-water has deposited in it? Of what use is the carbonate of lime in sea-water? What is said of common salt? What is the cause of the bitter taste of sea-water? What is said of solid matters in the water of rivers and lakes? Mention some inland lakes and seas that are salt. Why are they so? Give the experiment with the egg. Also the *experiment* with the toy ship.

CHAPTER XXVI.

SOLUTION AND CRYSTALLIZATION.

...is great difference in the different oxyds and salts in ...being dissolved. Some of them will not dissolve at all, ...ingly, and water will take in large quantities of some ... Calomel, for example, which is a chloride of mercury, is ...insoluble; that is, not a particle of it can be dissolved in ... But corrosive sublimate, the bichloride of mercury, is very ... Magnesia, an oxyd of the metal magnesium, is insoluble. ...this if you have ever taken calcined magnesia, as it is ...stirred up in sugar and water. But potash, which is an ...o, is exceedingly soluble. It is very eager for water, and ... will become dissolved in the water which it gathers ... air. It can be dissolved in half of its weight of water; ... pound of water will dissolve two pounds of potash. Now ... is another oxyd, likes water, but it takes a thousand ... of water to dissolve one pound of lime.

...Creator has made this great difference between potash and ...regard to solubility, because the difference is needed. For ... we want to use lime in plastering walls; but it would ... for this if it would, like potash, gather water from the ...dissolve in it. It would be rather inconvenient to have ...ing in our houses dissolve and run down whenever it ... wet. But for the uses for which man needs potash it is well to have it dissolve easily. For instance, it is used in making soap, and needs to be soluble for this purpose.

Salt dissolves easily, but not as easily as potash does. It would be inconvenient to have it do so. We want to keep salt dry for use, and this we could not do if it were as fond of water as potash is. The Creator has made it soluble to just the right degree to suit the uses for which he designed it. It sometimes troubles us by gathering moisture from the air, but this is only when the weather is damp; that is, when the air has much water in it.

Let us compare two carbonates in regard to solubility, the carbonate of soda and the carbonate of lime. The carbonate of soda is very soluble. This is convenient for the uses to which man puts this salt. But the carbonate of lime, which appears in the forms of chalk, limestome, marble, etc., is very sparingly soluble. It would be bad to have it dissolve readily in water. This salt, you know, makes the shells of oysters and other shell-fish. It would not be well to have their shell houses made of a material that the water could dissolve easily. And yet, if carbonate of lime were not somewhat soluble, how could it get into the blood of these animals so that it can be made into shell? You see, then, that the Creator has made this all just right.

But, besides this, it would be very injurious to have so much carbonate of lime in the water as there would be if it were very soluble. The rain that comes down upon chalk and limestone, which here and there form rocks and hills, and even mountains, washes down always a little, and carries it among the particles of the earth, and down streams into the ocean. That little is enough for building the houses of the shelled animals and other purposes.

...more soluble there would be more ... give us a great deal of trouble. When ... very commonly because there happens to ... of lime in it.

... of lime, sparingly soluble. Suppose ... soluble at all; all our grass and grain would lie ... for it is the silica in them that gives them ... which they stand up.

... when a substance is soluble, there will more dissolve ... cold water, but this is not so with common salt.

... have made water dissolve just as much of a substance ... it a *saturated* solution. This word comes from a ... which signifies to satisfy or feed to the full. Water ... satisfied or saturated with some substances than ... Potash and lime are in strong contrast in this re... a pound of water will not be satisfied till it has dis... of potash, while a thousand pounds of water will ... or saturated with a pound of lime; that is, it takes two ... as much potash to saturate water as it does lime.

... what it is to have a solid substance dissolved in water. ... substances you can mix up very thoroughly with wa... them well, and yet they do not dissolve. Cal... is readily mixed with water, but it is not dissolved, ... after the water has stood for a little while. But a ... that dissolves disappears. You can not see it. If it ... you see that in the water, but not the little grains or ... you do in the magnesia and water. A perfect solu... and transparent. The substance dissolved is much

There are great varieties in crystalline arrangement. I will point out some of them. In Fig. 52 you have represented a lump of mica. This is arranged in leaves which you can peel off exceedingly thin. You see this mineral used for windows in stove doors. The sheets of mica, or isinglass, as it is commonly called, used for this purpose, are really made up of very many of these thin leaves. In Fig. 53 you see the shapes of the crystals of common salt. They are exactly square blocks. And in Fig. 54 you see the forms of the crystals of a very beautiful mineral called calc spar, or sometimes Iceland spar, because it was first brought from Iceland. It is composed of the same things as common chalk. You see that the crystals are not square like those of salt, but they are sloping. These are but three of the very many varieties that occur in the shapes of crystals. Sometimes the same substance appears in many different forms. This is the case with gypsum, as noticed on page 137. The various forms and arrangements of the crystals of water in snow and frost are very beautiful. I have spoken of them particularly in the chapter on Snow, Frost, and Ice, in the Third Part of the Child's Book of Nature.

Fig. 52.

Fig. 53. Fig. 54.

In the crystals of some salts there is water locked up and concealed, but in some there is none. In carbonate of lime there is no water, but only carbonic acid and lime. In carbonate of soda, on the other hand, there is more of water than there is of carbonic [illegible] together. In 100 pounds of this salt there are 63 [illegible] the crystals are dry crystals; for the water is a [illegible] substance, locked up with the carbonic acid and [illegible] You can get this salt without any water in it by heat[illegible] the first thing it does on applying the heat is to melt [illegible] water. As you continue the heat you drive off this [illegible] the air, and the powder of the salt is left behind. It [illegible] crystalline; for it can not be so without its supply [illegible] its *water of crystallization*, as the chemists express it. [illegible] term is used in regard to any substance, we mean the [illegible] water which is contained by it when it is in a crystal[illegible] This differs in different substances. Some require [illegible] a little, and some a good deal.

[illegible] of potash, or saltpetre, has no water in it. If it had, it [illegible] answer as well for making gunpowder. Nitrate of [illegible] no water in it, and it would do for making gunpowder [illegible] the nitrate of potash, were it not for one thing: it gath[illegible] from the air. This would not answer for powder, [illegible] must be kept dry, you know. A salt which thus [illegible] moisture from the air is said to *deliquesce*—a word which [illegible] a Latin word meaning to melt. A salt, on the other [illegible], on exposure, loses its water of crystallization, and [illegible] from a crystal into a powder, is said to *effloresce*. Crys[illegible] do this have a mealy powder gradually form on their [illegible]. The word effloresce comes from the Latin word mean[illegible] flower. It is as if the mineral flowered out.

[illegible] the metals show us crystals. In the formation of the [illegible] described on page 142, the lead becomes crystalline.

carbonate has. People often use this [illegible] introducing some acid to take the potash, [illegible] gas may be set free and raise the dough. [illegible] ployed to decompose thus the sal eratus; [illegible]

When we separate carbonic acid from carbo[illegible] heat, very great heat is required. But we can [illegible] out any heat at all. It is by using an acid which [illegible] affinity for lime than the carbonic acid has. This [illegible] the mode of obtaining carbonic acid gas described [illegible] The muriatic acid takes the lime and lets the carbon[illegible] The same thing can be done with sulphuric acid, [illegible] greater affinity for lime than carbonic acid has.

Solid substances need commonly the help of water [illegible] their affinities for each other operate. If you mix the [illegible] ders, tartaric acid and bicarbonate of soda, together dry, [illegible] be no action; but if you dissolve them, as stated on page [illegible] soon as the solutions are mixed the tartaric acid at once takes hold of the soda, and the carbonic acid, thus released from the soda, effervesces. So, too, if you make a heap of the two powders mixed together, all will be quiet; but pour some water [illegible] the heap, and there will be a great disturbance as the water introduces the tartaric acid to the soda, and the carbonic acid [illegible] tice to quit. Why the difference? It is because in the dry state the two kinds of particles do not get near enough to each other to produce the effect. Powders, even when made very fine, look coarse when examined by the microscope; but the same substances dissolved in water are much more minutely divided, and so their particles are more thoroughly mixed up, and the [illegible] *to each other.*

You have seen that heat sometimes favors chemical affinity, and sometimes acts against it. Besides this, heat is often caused by chemical affinity. Generally, when any thing is burned, the heat which is produced is owing to the rapid union of oxygen with the burning substance. Thus, if carbon is burned, the carbon unites with oxygen, and so makes heat. The heat here comes from the affinity of carbon and oxygen for each other. So, when water and lime are mixed together, as in the making of mortar, great heat is produced by the action of the affinity. Sulphuric acid and water have a strong affinity for each other, and, as stated on page 119, when they are mingled together considerable heat is caused. In Fig. 55 you see represented a curious way of using this heat. Two men, who have gone up in a balloon so high that it is very cold, are hugging a bottle in which they have just mixed some sulphuric acid and water.

Fig. 55.

It is supposed that the heat in this case is owing to a good squeezing which the acid gives to the water, or which they give to each other. For if a pint of acid and a pint of water be poured together, the two pints make less than a quart; and this sudden condensation is supposed to create the heat.

Chemical affinity is exceedingly regular in its operations. It does not make substances unite in all sorts of proportions. If two substances unite together to form several different compounds, the proportions are so regular that they can be represented by whole numbers. I have already told you about this in regard to some compounds. For example, the bicarbonate of soda has exactly twice as much carbonic acid in it as the carbonate has (page 134), and the bichloride of mercury has twice as much chlorine as the chloride. So, too, in the five compounds of oxygen and nitrogen (page 29), the proportions of oxygen are exactly as 1, 2, 3, 4, and 5.

Observe now, in regard to the compounds of oxygen and nitrogen, that the nitrogen is the same in amount in all of them. The difference of proportion is only in the oxygen. Of the five compounds there is the most oxygen in the nitric acid, and the least in the nitrous oxyd or laughing gas. In the nitrous oxyd the proportion of oxygen is as 8 to 14; that is, in 22 pounds of nitrous oxyd there are 8 of oxygen and 14 of nitrogen. But as in nitric acid there is the same amount of nitrogen, but five times as much oxygen, the proportion of oxygen to nitrogen in this acid is as 40 to 14; that is, while there are 8 pounds of oxygen and 14 of nitrogen in 22 of nitrous oxyd, there are 40 of oxygen and only 14 of nitrogen in 54 of nitric acid. Can you tell me, then, how much there is of oxygen and of nitrogen in 108 pounds of nitric acid? If you work out the following sums by the rule of three, you will get the right answers.

54 : 40 : : 108 : amount of the oxygen.
54 : 14 : : 108 : amount of the nitrogen.

The proportions of the different compounds of oxygen and nitrogen may be stated thus:

	Nitrogen.	Oxygen.
Nitrous oxyd	14	8
Nitric oxyd	14	16
Hyponitrous acid	14	24
Nitrous acid	14	32
Nitric acid	14	40

The difference in the proportion of oxygen, you see, is exactly as 1, 2, 3, 4, and 5. There is never the least variation from this. You can not in any way make, for example, 8½ pounds of oxygen unite with 14 of nitrogen. The extra half pound will be put one side. The 14 pounds of nitrogen will not take a jot more than 8 of oxygen. To make it unite with any more, you must give it twice as much, 16 pounds, and then it will make nitric oxyd; or 24, and then it will make hyponitrous acid, and so on.

There are some substances that unite in a different range of proportions—1, 1½, 2, 3, 3½. But this can not be really called an irregularity.

Compounds differ from mere mixtures in these fixed and definite proportions. You can mix alcohol and water together in all kinds of proportions. The same is true of the mixtures of the metals called alloys; but in forming real compounds, substances unite together in exact proportions.

We see in this exactness of proportions, as we do in crystallization, what order prevails in creation. Nothing is left loose and indefinite, as is too often the case with many of the arrangements of man. Amid all the changes of matter, whether taking place in quiet, or in the agitation of combustion, or even explosion, there is always in the combinations that occur a strict compliance with the arithmetical proportions that I have indicated. God thus marshals in perfect order alike minute particles and immense worlds.

Questions.—What is chemical affinity? State the difference in strength of affinity of iron and potassium for oxygen. What is said of the quick union of iron with oxygen? How is the affinity of iron for oxygen illustrated in one mode of obtaining hydrogen? What is said of the noble metals? Give what is stated in Chapter IV. about the union of nitrogen and oxygen. What is said of the affinity of phosphorus for oxygen? What is the object of putting chlorate of potash with phosphorus in matches? Give an example of heat acting in opposition to chemical affinity. What is said of decomposing carbonate of potash? What is decomposition? What is said of the bicarbonate of potash? What is said of separating carbonic acid from carbonate of lime? What is said of the influence of water on chemical affinity? State what is said about mixing soda powders. Give some examples of heat being produced by chemical affinity. Explain Fig. 55. What really produces the heat in this case? What is said of the regularity with which chemical affinity acts? State particularly what is said of the compounds of nitrogen and oxygen. How much oxygen and how much nitrogen is there in 108 pounds of nitric acid? How much in 162 pounds? How much in 100? in 60? in 25? State what is said about the exactness of the proportions of oxygen in the different compounds of oxygen and nitrogen. What different range of proportions is there in some cases? How do compounds differ from mixtures in regard to proportions? What is said of the order preserved in creation?

CHAPTER XXVIII.

WOOD.

So far I have told you mostly about the chemistry of *mineral* substances; that is, substances which neither have life in them nor are produced by the operations of life. Most people, when the term mineral substances is used, think only of solid substances; but air and water are as really minerals as the crystals you see in a cabinet of minerals, or the rocks and stones that you see about you. Wood, sugar, starch, gum, skin, flesh, etc., on the other hand, are not mineral, for some of these have life, and all of them are produced only by the operations of life in either vegetables or animals. It is to this chemistry of life, as we may call it, that we shall attend in the few remaining chapters. I shall begin with the chemistry of vegetables.

I have told you already something about the chemistry of vegetables in speaking of carbon as entering into the leaves and making a part of the wood of trees. Now wood is composed of three things, carbon, oxygen, and hydrogen. You see that it is composed of a solid united with two gases. When we make charcoal out of wood, as I described to you on page 38, we decompose the wood. We send off its oxygen and hydrogen into the air by the heat of the burning, and most of the carbon is left behind alone. I say most of it, but not all, for some of the carbon unites with the oxygen in the combustion, and flies off as carbonic acid gas.

Although you can thus decompose wood, you can not take the

ingredients and unite them together so as to make wood of them. If you mix up powdered charcoal with water, you have all of the ingredients of wood together; but you can not in any way make them unite together to form wood. So you have the ingredients of wood if you put charcoal into a jar filled with oxygen and hydrogen gases, but they will not turn into wood; they will remain just so. If you light up the charcoal before you put it into the jar, an effect will be produced, but no wood will be made; an explosion will take place, the oxygen and hydrogen uniting together in a great hurry, forming water, and some of the oxygen uniting with the charcoal to form carbonic acid gas. So, again, if you take carbonic acid gas and mingle it in a jar with hydrogen gas, you have the three ingredients of wood, carbon, oxygen, and hydrogen, but they will not unite to make wood.

See how different this is from what we can do with some of the minerals that I have told you about. For example, take sulphate of copper or blue vitriol: this is composed of three things, sulphur, oxygen, and copper. Now we can make the sulphur and oxygen unite to form sulphuric acid, and then this acid will unite with the copper, forming the sulphate of copper. How readily, as another example, carbon and oxygen unite, and make carbonic acid, and then the acid unites with the lime to form the carbonate, chalk.

But, although *we* can not in any way make the ingredients of wood unite to form wood, it is done in the tree. Let us see how. Much of the carbon is furnished from the air, being taken in by the leaves from the air, as you learned in Chapter VIII. Then the water that comes up in the sap from the roots furnishes the [illegible] and hydrogen, for water, you know, is composed of these [illegible]. We may say, then, that the tree makes its own wood [illegible] charcoal and water.

[illegible] in every tree, is composed of the same things, carbon, [illegible] and hydrogen, although the trees are so different; and [illegible] more difference in the ways in which wood is put togeth-[illegible] different trees than you would suppose from looking at the [illegible], or from seeing the wood itself with the naked eye. The [illegible]scope shows astonishing differences. In order to see these, [illegible]ingly thin shavings, of various kinds of wood, are cut with [illegible] sharp instrument across the grain of the wood. On ex-[illegible] these with the microscope, they are so much magnified [illegible] we can see just how each kind of wood is put together. In [illegible], as the pine, there is a very open network, with here and [illegible] large round openings, while in other more solid woods the [illegible] are much less. These spaces have very great variety of [illegible]ngement in different kinds of wood, and in some the arrange-[illegible] is exceedingly beautiful.

[illegible] in mind the fact that in all these varieties we have [illegible] the same thing in composition, is there any thing that you [illegible] remember of what I have told you that is somewhat like [illegible]? Can you recollect any mineral substance that appears in [illegible] forms, and yet in composition is the same in all these [illegible], as the wood is in its forms? I will mention one, gypsum, [illegible] on page 137, and perhaps you can remember some others.

But there is still more variety in wood than I have yet told [illegible] about. There are a great many other things which are real-[illegible] wood besides those which people commonly call by this name.

The bark of trees is wood, only in a different form from the wood which it covers, very much as chalk or the common limestone differs from marble. Hold a leaf up so that the light can shine through it. All that delicate frame-work that you see is a wooden frame-work. More than this, the skin of the leaf and all its filling up are wood. The whole leaf is wood except the sap that is in it, and that which gives it its beautiful color; and what I have said of leaves is true also of flowers. The most delicate flower that you can find is made of wood—very, very fine and delicate is such wood, and yet it is wood.

You see a hyacinth growing at the window in a glass vessel in which there is nothing but water. The plant that grows up from the hyacinth bulb is little else than wood filled out in all its cells with water. See how this wood is formed. The water furnishes the oxygen and hydrogen, and the carbon comes from the air.

Every stalk of grain and spire of grass is made mostly of wood. In both of these cases we have fine particles of flint scattered all along in the wood to make it firm enough to stand up in spite of the wind.

Much of the clothing that you wear is nothing but wood. You can hardly believe this; but so it is. A shirt, whether it be made of cotton or linen, is a wooden shirt. Cotton or linen fibre is woody fibre. It is composed of carbon, oxygen, and hydrogen in exactly the same proportions with what we commonly call wood.

You remember that I told you in a previous chapter about the old-fashioned tinder-box. Charred or scorched linen was always used in the box to catch the spark from the steel. This is really charcoal made from the linen, just as we make charcoal from pieces of wood—that is, by a partial burning. It was used for this purpose instead of common charcoal because it is so fine in its division into fibres that the spark very readily sets fire to it.

All paper is wood. It is made, when it is fine, as writing-paper, of cotton and linen rags, and these are wood. If you tear a sheet of letter-paper, and look at the torn edge through a magnifying glass or a microscope, you will see very plainly the woody fibres pointing out in all directions from the edge. In paper these fibres are not regularly arranged as in the cotton after it is gathered, but they are mingled together in all sorts of ways, lying across each other in confusion.

All the frame-work, as we may call it, of fruits is wood. All the partitions in fruits are wooden partitions. The orange, you know, is divided into several parts by partitions. These are made of wood. Besides this, the juice of an orange is inclosed in thousands and thousands of little bottles, and these bottles are wooden bottles. The next time you eat an orange, observe them. See how pretty they are, and how nicely they are packed in each of the parts of the orange. Their large rounded ends are toward the peal, and their slender pointed ends are toward the middle of the orange. When you eat an orange you crush a multitude of these wooden bottles, and the juice runs out of them into your mouth. And so, when you eat any juicy fruit, you break up wooden apartments or cells that hold the fluid. Even in the most juicy fruits there is some wood all through them, and the skins or coverings of the fruits are made of wood.

The coverings of all seeds are wooden. In some of the nuts the woody substance forming their covering is very dense and hard, as in the cocoanut, the walnut. The substance called vegetable ivory is wood very closely put together.

The very delicate forms in which woody substance sometimes appears remind us of the fine crystals in which some minerals sometimes show themselves. Thus saltpetre, which is commonly rather a coarse-looking mineral, is sometimes seen on the walls of caverns in fine, needle-like crystals; and, to take another example of a more familiar character, the delicate tracing of the frost on our windows is but another form or arrangement of the same material that we have in thick ice.

Questions.—What is the difference between substances which are mineral and those which are not? What have you already learned about the chemistry of vegetables? What is said about the composition of wood? What is done to wood in making charcoal? What is said about making wood? Give the contrast to this in regard to minerals. How is wood formed in the tree? What is said of the different forms of wood in different kinds of trees? Give the comparison in relation to this. What is said of leaves and flowers? What of the hyacinth? What of grain and grass? What of clothing? What of tinder? What of paper? What of fruits? Describe the arrangement of the orange. What is said of the coverings of seeds? What is vegetable ivory? Give the comparison in relation to the delicate forms of wood.

CHAPTER XXIX.

STARCH AND SUGAR.

Starch is a very common substance in vegetables. It is not so common as wood, for that, as you have seen, is every where, in every part of all vegetables, from the largest trees to the smallest plants. There is some starch in all the vegetable substances that we eat. In some kinds there is a great deal of starch. Four fifths of the flour of which our bread is made is starch. Most of the potato is starch. There is much of it in chestnuts, and even in horse-chestnuts it constitutes one eighth of the whole. Arrow-root is a starchy meal, prepared from some plants that grow in marshy grounds in warm climates, as the East and West Indies. Sago is a starchy substance, prepared from the pith of various kinds of palm-trees. From all this you see that a large part of the food of man is starch.

You can very readily obtain starch from wheat flour. Moisten a handful of it with enough water to make a thin paste. Put this into a piece of thick linen cloth and knead it, adding water to the paste as long as the liquid which runs through the cloth appears milky. Let the liquid in the vessel stand for some time, and a white powder will settle at the bottom. This is wheat starch. What remains in the cloth I will tell you about in the next chapter.

¶ The starch is in grains, and each little grain, as seen by the microscope, has a covering. Now in boiling starch we swell it up into a thick jelly. In this operation the coatings of the grains are broken, and the starch absorbs considerable water. This is the reason that rice, beans, barley, etc., swell so much when they are cooked. Your chestnuts swell when you boil them from the same cause.

You will be surprised to learn that starch, though so different from wood, is composed of the same elements, carbon, hydrogen, and oxygen, and that, too, in the same proportions. It is deposited in those parts of the plant where it can be used for food, as grains or seeds, and other fruits, as the tubers of the potato-plant.

Sugar is another substance which is found in many plants. All fruits that are sweet have sugar in them. Besides this, there are some plants which are designed by the Creator to make sugar for the use of man; of these the principal is the sugar-cane. Then there is the sugar-maple and the sugar-beet. Much sugar is obtained from the sugar-maple in the northern parts of this country. On the Continent of Europe, especially in France, the sugar-beet is largely cultivated for the manufacture of sugar.

Sugar, like starch and wood, is composed of carbon, oxygen, and hydrogen, but not in the same proportions. Although we can not make sugar by mixing these ingredients together, any more than we can wood or starch, yet this is done in plants. The sugar-cane makes sugar for us out of charcoal and water, as I have told you wood is made. Much of the charcoal or carbon is taken from the air by the leaves, while the water comes up from the ground by the roots. The long, broad leaves, shaped much like corn-leaves, are spread out to the air to suck in, by their little and numberless mouths, the carbon from the air, so that there may be

... of this material for making the sugar. Now as the carbonic gas comes in part from the breath of animals, it may be ... of the carbon in some of the sugar that you have eaten ... came from your lungs. If so, a long way did it fly, on ... of the wind, to the South, to get to the cane-leaf that ...

... obtaining sugar from the cane, the juice is first pressed out ... heavy iron rollers. This juice is then cleared mostly of ... and is boiled down to such a degree that the sugar ... crystallize as it cools. While this crystallization is going on, ... draining off of a sirup, and this is molasses. The sugar ... in grains, and is the common brown sugar. Farther ... is required to make it into white sugar.

... are different kinds of sugar. The two most important I ... —grape-sugar and cane-sugar. Grape-sugar is that ... is in grapes and in sweet fruits generally. Cane-sugar is ... which is in sugar-cane and other plants that are evidently ... by the Creator to manufacture sugar for our use. The ... sugar has much greater sweetening power than grape-sugar, ... therefore is more valuable. It requires almost three tea... of grape-sugar to sweeten as much as a single teaspoon... of the cane-sugar.

... difference in composition between these two kinds is that ... -sugar has more of oxygen and hydrogen than the cane-... or, because oxygen and hydrogen are the two ingredients ..., some chemists say that grape-sugar has more water in ... the other.

... we can not take carbon, and oxygen, and hydrogen,

N

Sugar made from saw-dust.

and make them into wood, or starch, or sugar, we can [illegible] ar out of either starch or wood. What! you will [illegible] claim, make sugar out of saw-dust? Yes, exactly so [illegible] done by oil of vitriol, water, and heat. Every five pounds [illegible] kinds of wood may be made to give us in this way four [illegible]

The process is as follows: The saw-dust is first moistened [illegible] a little more than its weight of sulphuric acid or oil of vitriol, and is left to stand for about twelve hours. It is now [illegible] dry; but, on pounding it in a mortar, it becomes liquid. [illegible] water is added, and it is boiled. The sugar is now formed.

The explanation of its formation is this. In the saw-dust there are certain quantities of carbon, oxygen, and hydrogen, [illegible] there is not so much of the oxygen and hydrogen as there is in sugar. What needs to be done, then, in order to make the wood into sugar, is to add some oxygen and hydrogen, letting the carbon be just as it is. This is exactly what the sulphuric acid does. It forces some of the water, or the oxygen and hydrogen that compose it, to unite with the carbon in the saw-dust, and so sugar is made.

But the sugar is not alone. It is a sirup; that is, there is water mixed with it. Besides this, the sulphuric acid is there also. This acid does not become a part of the sugar. It only forces some of the water to unite with the carbon of the wood. The acid itself is unchanged, and there it is mingled with the sirup. It would not do to let it remain, for you know how biting an acid it is. The way in which it is taken out of the sirup is a good example of chemical affinity. Chalk will take it out. See how it does this. Chalk is carbonate of lime. Now sulphuric acid likes [illegible] carbonic acid does. It therefore takes the lime, [illegible] acid flies off. The sulphuric acid forms with [illegible] sulphate of lime or gypsum. As this does not dissolve [illegible] the sirup is very easily separated from it.

[illegible] have the sirup. To get the sugar we have only to [illegible] sirup, and thus drive off the water into the air.

[illegible] can be manufactured from rags as easily as from wood; [illegible] you learned in the previous chapter, the rags are nothing [illegible] wood in a certain form.

[illegible] process of converting starch into sugar is essentially the [illegible] starch has the same composition as wood, as you learned [illegible] first part of this chapter. But what is the sugar that can [illegible] made out of such cheap materials as saw-dust and rags? [illegible] the cane-sugar, which is so valuable, but the grape-sug[illegible] If we could manufacture cane-sugar in this way, we should [illegible] to depend so entirely on the sugar-cane for our supply.

[illegible] how singular it is that grape-sugar is formed instead of [illegible] To form the cane-sugar the sulphuric acid would have to [illegible] water to unite with the carbon to only one quarter the [illegible] which must be added to make the grape-sugar. It would [illegible] it would be easier to make the less quantity unite with [illegible] than the greater. But no one has ever yet discov[illegible] way of doing this. If any one could make such a dis[illegible], and so manufacture cane-sugar out of saw-dust and rags, [illegible] would make him richer than the richest man now liv[illegible] perhaps the richest that ever lived.

[illegible] England and on the Continent of Europe, where sugar is [illegible] cheap as it is in this country, there has been a great deal of cheating done by making this rag and saw-dust sugar and mixing it with the sweeter cane-sugar. In England there is a law forbidding the manufacture of the grape-sugar.

I have told you that there is sugar in all sweet fruits, but there is not sugar in them at first. They are either tasteless or acid, and become sweet as they ripen. Before they ripen there is starch in them, and this changes into sugar. Some of the acid also changes into this substance.

Though we can make wood into sugar, we can not turn sugar into wood. This is done, however, in plants. Suppose we have a sugar-maple that has not been tapped by any one, what becomes of all the sugar that is in it in the spring? Does it stay there locked up for some one to get next spring? If it does, what a quantity of sugar there will be for him, for he will have all that is made in two springs. But the sugar does not all stay there as sugar. It circulates about in the tree, and helps to make leaves, and bark, and wood. This seems strange to you. But that sugar should be turned into wood is no more strange than that wood should turn into sugar; and yet this last I have told you that we could effect with heat and oil of vitriol. And when we come to look into the whole matter, it is not so strange after all, for wood and sugar are both composed of the same things, carbon, oxygen, and hydrogen. The proportions only need to be altered to change the one into the other.

We see the same change of sugar into wood in other vegetables. Thus the sugar-beet and turnip are sweetest when gathered early. If allowed to remain growing too long, the sugar is changed into wood, and they become, therefore, tough and taste-

[illegible] So, also, if grape [illegible] the starch and sugar in [illegible] wood, [illegible] as sweet and nutritious as it would have been if produced [illegible]

We can make charcoal from sugar as we do from wood, for it is composed of the same elements that wood is. We can do it simply by heating the sugar. But a prettier way to do it is this: Put a tablespoonful of strong sirup, made with loaf-sugar, into a tumbler set in a large plate, and pour upon it a little good sulphuric acid. The acid sets free the charcoal, producing considerable heat. This makes a [illegible] bubbling up, even over the sides of the tumbler. After the tumbler gets cool, pour the contents into the plate, and you have a specimen of *sugar-charcoal*.

Questions.—What is said of the abundance of starch in plants? Mention some of the vegetable substances in which it is found. What is arrow-root? what sago? How can you obtain starch from wheaten flour? What sort of a substance is starch? What effect has boiling upon it? What is said of the composition of starch? Where in plants is it deposited? What is said of the presence of sugar in vegetables? What is the composition of sugar? What is said about the making of sugar in plants? What about your breath furnishing sugar-making plants with carbon? How is sugar obtained from the sugar-cane? What is molasses? What are the two kinds of sugar, and how do they differ? What is their difference in composition? What is said of making sugar from wood and starch? Describe the process of making it out of wood. Explain the chemistry of the process. How, now, is the sulphuric acid got rid of? How is the dry sugar obtained from the sirup? What is said of making rags into sugar? What of making sugar from starch? What kind of sugar is made from these substances? What is said of not being able to make cane-sugar in this way? What of the manufacture of grape sugar in Europe? What is said about the formation of sugar in fruits? What about the change of sugar into wood in the sugar-maple? What about the same change in vegetables? What is said of sugar-charcoal?

CHAPTER XXX.

GLUTEN.

YOU see that vegetable substances are made [illegible] oxygen, and hydrogen; but animal substances, flesh, [illegible] nerves, etc., are made of these same three things, but with [illegible] added, viz., nitrogen. It is this gas that makes the [illegible] tion between animal and most vegetable substances. [illegible] substance was ever found that had no nitrogen in it. [illegible]

It is the nitrogen that gives the peculiar strong odor [illegible] smell whenever any animal substance is burned. Wood, [illegible] linen, etc., give out but little smell when burned, but let [illegible] en thing, or hair, or leather be burned, and the odor is [illegible] able and strong, and it is very much the same in all [illegible]

As all substances which are peculiar to animals have [illegible] in them, there must, of course, be some nitrogen in their food, [illegible] without this they would droop and die. It is the food [illegible] the blood, and the blood, as you learned in the Second Part of the Child's Book of Nature, is the building and repairing material [illegible] the body. You can see, then, that if no nitrogen is furnished [illegible] the blood, one of the four great materials for building and [illegible] ing will soon be spent. The body will, therefore, in a little [illegible] show this great want, and get out of repair. And, if it [illegible] long, it will die. To repair the body without nitrogen would [illegible] very much like repairing a brick wall without brick, [illegible] breaches in it with mortar alone.

... can readily see where some animals get that part of ... building and repairing material which we call nitrogen. ... dogs, cats, etc., eat animal food, and there is nitro... always in that. But how is it with horses, cows, sheep, etc.? ... do they get their nitrogen? They eat no animal food, ... vegetable substances that I have told you about, wood, ... and sugar, have no nitrogen in them. There is a plenty ... all around them in the air, and they breathe it con... into their lungs. Do they get it in this way? No, not ... of the nitrogen gas that goes into the lungs gets into the ... The oxygen that goes into the lungs with the nitrogen ... the blood, but the nitrogen does not. It comes out of the ... exactly the same as when it went in. Neither does a particle ... nitrogen go into the body of animals through the skin, though ... is bathed in it all the time.

... then, do the vegetable-eating animals get their nitrogen? ... tell you. You remember that, in telling you how to obtain ... from wheat flour, I said that there was a substance left in ... cloth; it is mostly a substance which we call *gluten*—a ... glutinous or sticky substance. This portion of the flour con... nitrogen. While the starchy part is composed of carbon, ... and hydrogen, this is composed of these and nitrogen ... with them.

... the gluten of the flour that gives firmness to bread. If it ... composed of starch alone the bread would be very crumbling. ... this reason that rice griddle-cakes so readily break when ... not enough flour mingled with the rice. The gluten of ... flour is needed to hold together the starchy rice.

There is another substance in the flour [illegible] It is called *albumen*, from the Latin word *albus*, [illegible] the white of egg, and is really about the same thing [illegible] but little of it in the flour compared with the gluten [illegible]

In the grain of wheat, then, we have three substances [illegible] gluten, and albumen. There is much more of starch [illegible] ten, and the albumen is very small in amount.

There is another substance that has nitrogen in it [illegible] found in many vegetables. We call it *casein*. It is [illegible] same thing as the cheese which is contained in all milk, [illegible] makes the curd. There is a great deal of this substance in [illegible] tables that grow in pods, as peas, beans, etc.

The three substances in vegetables that furnish animals [illegible] nitrogen are, then, gluten, albumen, and casein. They are [illegible] *nitrogenous* substances. The most abundant of them is [illegible] There is a great deal of this in the grains which are used [illegible] tensively for food—wheat, rye, buckwheat, barley, oats, Indian corn, etc.

Starch and sugar have no nitrogen in them, and carbon is [illegible] most important element. They are said, therefore, to be *carbonaceous* substances, in distinction from the nitrogenous. Now these substances can not support life for any length of time alone. Some dogs which, by way of experiment, were fed upon nothing but starch and sugar, languished and died. It was for want of nitrogen.

There is another class of substances, found both in vegetables and animals, which are carbonaceous, and have no nitrogen in them. They are the oils and fats.

It is the nitrogenous substances in our food that build up and repair the body. Of what use, then, are starch, sugar, and the fats? Their use is chiefly, if not wholly, to keep up the heat of the body. They are a part of the fuel, which is burning up every where with the oxygen that is in the blood, as you learned in the chapter on Animal Heat.

The power of an article of food to nourish the body or promote its growth is supposed to depend on the amount of nitrogen there is in it. Rice is not very nutritious, because it contains a great deal of starch and very little gluten. The common grains, as wheat, rye, etc., are among the most nutritious vegetable articles, for there is much gluten in them. There is a great deal in the coverings of the grains, which, broken up, make the bran. Therefore bread made from bolted flour is not as nutritious as that which is made from the unbolted flour. Peas and beans are very nutritious, because they contain so much of that nitrogenous substance, casein, or vegetable cheese. Cabbage is one of the most nutritious of vegetables, for it has even more gluten in it than the grains; and cauliflower has a still greater supply of it than the cabbage.

There is some gluten in leaves and grass, but not so much as in the grains. The horse, therefore, though he may do pretty well upon hay alone when idle, must have some kind of grain when he is worked. The wear and tear of the muscles in working makes a good supply of nitrogenous food necessary for repair. The camelopard, with his long neck, lives by browsing upon the leaves of trees. But if he worked, like the horse, he would require some food richer in gluten.

For the same reason, the food of a laboring man should be richer in gluten than that of a man who lives at his ease. In the repairing that his muscles require after the wear and tear of labor, it will not do to supply only food that is composed of carbon, and oxygen, and hydrogen, with very little or no nitrogen. There must be a good quantity of nitrogen in his food; for this is quite as essential as the other materials. If the laborer, therefore, should live chiefly on rice, as in China, or on potatoes, as is often the case in Ireland, the machinery of his body would not be well repaired, and he would become weak. He must have such food as bread and meat, with his potatoes, rice, etc., in order to get enough nitrogen for growth and repair.

We need to have mingled together the two kinds of food—that which is for building and that which is for fuel. It is for this reason that the fuel-food, pork, goes well with the building-food, cabbage.

Those articles in which the two kinds of food are mingled together are peculiarly good articles. Thus bread is so good that it is called the staff of life. Still better is it when we add to it the fatty carbonaceous substance, butter. Milk is such a combination of the nitrogenous and carbonaceous substances that it is a *complete* food by itself, as shown by the fact that children often live a long time on this article alone.

I have told you that all animal substances have nitrogen in them, and that most vegetable substances do not. Still there are some vegetable substances that do contain nitrogen. Why do they contain it? It is for the very purpose of supplying it to animals. Animals must have it in their structures—in their mus-

...es, bones, skin, brain, etc. But vegetables do not need ... structures. Wood does very well without it, though ... muscle can not. As, then, vegetables do not need it in ... structures, Providence does not put it there, but makes it go ... of vegetables where animals can readily get at it, and ... their food. It is for this purpose that there is so much ... deposited in various grains for the use of man and other animals.

...—Of what are most vegetable substances composed? What compose ... substances? What distinguishes animal from most vegetable substances? ... said of the odor of animal substances in burning? What is said of the ne... of having some nitrogen in the food of animals? In regard to what animals is ... where they get their nitrogen? What is said about the vegetable-eaters ... it from the air? What is said about gluten? What about the gluten ...? What about rice cakes? What is said of albumen? What of the three ... in the grain of wheat? What is said of casein? What are *nitroge*... vegetable substances? Which is the most abundant of them? What are *car*... vegetable substances? What is said of their power to support life? What ... oils and fats? Of what special use are starch, sugar, and the fats? Upon ... the nourishing power of substances depend? What is said of the grains ... respect? What of unbolted flour? What of peas and beans? What of ... and cauliflowers? What is said of animals being able to live on grass? ... the camelopard? What of the necessity of nitrogenous food for the labor...? What about having the two kinds of food mingled? What is said of ...? What of milk? What is said, in conclusion, about nitrogen in animals ... vegetables?

CHAPTER XXXI.

FERMENTATION.

In the two previous chapters I have told you about some substances which are found in vegetables—starch, sugar, gluten, etc. In this chapter I shall tell you about some substances which are made from these by man.

You have heard the word *ferment* often used, but have you ever thought exactly what it means? When cider is first made, it is the mere juice of the apples. It is not fermented. It works or ferments afterward. So, also, wine is the fermented juice of grapes. In making it, the juice has worked or fermented, as the juice of apples does in turning to cider. Wine is made in the same way from other fruits, as currant, gooseberry, etc. When people use the word wine alone, it is understood as meaning grape-wine. When other wines are spoken of, the name of the fruit from which it was made is always given.

What is done by the fermentation? What is the change that is produced? It is a change in the proportions of carbon, oxygen, and hydrogen, of which the substances that ferment are composed, or, rather, it is a change in one of these substances. The substance which is changed is sugar. All those liquids which become intoxicating drinks by fermentation are composed chiefly of sugar dissolved in water, having a flavor given to it by the plant from which it comes. Thus the change produced in the juice of apples is only in the sugar that is in it. The water in [illegible] the sugar is dissolved is not changed at all, neither is that [illegible] gives the peculiar taste to cider in distinction from other [illegible]ing drinks. So, also, grape-juice is sugar dissolved in [illegible] with a flavor peculiar to the grape, and it is the sugar only [illegible] changed in the fermentation.

[illegible] now what the change produced in the sugar is. The [illegible] sweet to the taste, is changed into a fiery substance call[illegible]ohol. It is so fiery that it must be diluted before it can [illegible]. In the strongest wine there is three times as much [illegible] there is alcohol; more than half of the strongest brandy [illegible]; in common beer only the one fiftieth part is alcohol.

[illegible] have not yet told you precisely what the chemical change [illegible] fermentation produces in the sugar. Sugar is composed [illegible], hydrogen, and oxygen in certain proportions. It is [illegible] in these proportions that turns the sugar into alcohol. [illegible]ohol is composed, as sugar is, of carbon, oxygen, and hy[illegible], but their proportions are altered. It is just as calomel [illegible]rosive sublimate differ from each other, the proportions [illegible] their ingredients, chlorine and mercury, being different, [illegible] on page 162. It is also as the difference is made be[illegible] laughing gas and the biting nitric acid.

[illegible] change of proportions, nothing is added to the sugar to [illegible] into alcohol. Something, on the other hand, is taken [illegible] Some of the carbon and some of the oxygen of the sugar [illegible] forming carbonic acid gas, which flies off into the air, if [illegible]mitted to do so. The alcohol has as much hydrogen as [illegible] from which it is formed, but has less carbon and oxy-

You see that the fermentation produces two things from the sugar—alcohol and carbonic acid. The sugar is divided or split into these.

What produces this change in the sugar? Does the sugar change of itself? No; the change in the sugar is caused by something else. If you make a solution of sugar in perfectly pure water, it will never turn into alcohol. Something must be added to the solution to effect this change. If you put in a little yeast, this will do it. But how? Does the yeast unite with anything in the sugar to form the alcohol, as oxygen unites with iron to form rust, or with potassium to form potash? No; it simply forces the sugar to separate into two things, carbonic acid and alcohol. The yeast does not become a part of either the carbonic acid or the alcohol, just as the sulphuric acid, in changing wood into sugar (page 194), does not become a part of the sugar. It is merely the instrument by which the sugar is split into two parts, and is itself unchanged.

But we do not put yeast into the juice of the grape to turn it into wine, or into the juice of the apple to turn it into cider. How, then, is the alcohol formed in them? There is some gluten in these juices, and this becomes yeast, and so produces the fermentation. Either one of the nitrogenous substances, gluten, albumen, or casein, may act as a ferment. Common cheese may be used, for this is but a form of casein.

The fermentation of bread is really the same thing with the fermentation which produces intoxicating drinks. The yeast turns the sugar that is in the dough into alcohol and carbonic acid, and these two together swell out the hollow cells which grow [illegible] the bread. But you will ask what becomes of the alcohol. [illegible] off in vapor in the oven, and escapes into the air. In [illegible] large bakeries, in Europe, an attempt has been made to [illegible] this vapor and condense it, so as to save the alcohol; but it [illegible] been very successful.

[illegible] uncorking bottles of Champagne wine and cider there is a [illegible] escape of gas, making a lively foam. This gas is carbonic [illegible]. It is made in the bottle by fermentation, and, so long [illegible] liquid is confined by a tight cork, the gas is imprisoned [illegible] among the particles of the liquid; but, the moment the [illegible] loosened, the gas escapes. In order to have this gas pro-[illegible] the liquid is put into the bottles before the fermentation is [illegible]. A part of the process, therefore, goes on in the bottle, [illegible] the gas. The same thing is true of bottled beer.

[illegible] production of alcohol from the grains, barley, rye, etc., and [illegible] potatoes, is different from its production from apple-juice [illegible] grape-juice. In the articles which I have mentioned there [illegible] deal of starch and but little sugar, and this starch must [illegible] changed into sugar before alcohol can be produced. Thus, [illegible] making beer from barley, the first thing is to make as much as [illegible] of the starch in the barley into sugar. It is done in this [illegible]. The grain is moistened and left in heaps; it sprouts, and, [illegible] this, much of the starch is turned into sugar, so that the [illegible] has a very sweet taste. The *malt*, for so this sugared bar-[illegible] called, is now dried, and, after being bruised, is put into the [illegible] with water; after boiling sufficiently, the liquor is drawn [illegible]. It is now a sugary solution, and, the yeast being [illegible] it, produces the alcohol from the sugar, just as it does

from the sugar of grape-juice in making wine, or that of apple-juice in making cider. When the mixture is boiling, the hops are put in to give the bitter flavor.

So, also, in making whisky from the potato, the starch must first be converted into sugar.

As alcoholic liquor is produced from the fermentation of a sugary solution, so vinegar is produced from the fermentation of an alcoholic liquor. The change which is effected in this case is the addition of oxygen to the alcohol, forming acetic acid, the acid of vinegar. As iron-rust is oxydized iron, and potash is oxydized potassium, so acetic acid is oxydized alcohol. If we leave a barrel of cider with its bung-hole open, it gradually becomes vinegar, because the oxygen of the air comes to the alcohol in it and oxydizes it.

It is not the whole of the cider that is changed. As, when apple-juice turns to cider, it is only the sugar in the juice that is changed, so, when the cider becomes vinegar, the change is only in the alcohol. This turns to acetic acid, and what we call vinegar is only a little of this acid diffused through considerable water, as noticed on page 122.

As the sugar will not change of itself into alcohol, so the alcohol will not change of itself into vinegar; there must be a ferment or yeast to produce this fermentation as well as that which forms alcohol. In making vinegar from cider in the common way, the work is done by the same gluten that was in the apple-juice and turned it into cider.

Sometimes vinegar is manufactured in a rapid manner. It is done in barrels, as seen in Fig. 56. The barrel is represented in

Fig. 56.

the figure as being open, that you may understand the arrangement. A mixture of alcohol and water, having a little yeast in it, is put into the vessel *b*, and is allowed to drip from it through small holes in the bottom. The barrel is filled with loose shavings, which have been steeped in vinegar. The air is admitted through holes *c*, *c*, *c*. Observe what the chemical operation of this is. The oxygen of the air unites with the alcohol as it trickles down through the shavings, and oxydizes it or turns it into vinegar. The vinegar is collected in a receiver, *a*. The object of the loose shavings is to spread out, as we may say, the alcohol, so that the air can come freely to every particle of it.

The circulation of the air among the shavings is made very free by the heat which is produced by the process. This causes an upward current of air through the barrel, for the same reason that a fire in a fireplace causes an upward current in a chimney. Think a moment of the cause of this heat. The oxydation of the alcohol is a real combustion or burning, like all other oxydation, as stated in the chapter on Combustion. It produces heat, though not enough to cause a flame, for the oxydation is not rapid enough for that.

In this chapter I have told you about some substances which never are found in plants, but which can be made out of certain vegetable substances. Thus, alcohol is never made in any plant, but man finds sugar in many plants, and out of that makes alcohol. Then out of this he makes the acid of vinegar, ether, and some other substances.

Now, as you can not make wood by mixing in any way its ingredients (page 186), so you can not make alcohol out of its ingredients. The only way to make it is to decompose sugar. So, also, you can not make the acid of vinegar, acetic acid, by mixing up its components. It is composed, like alcohol, of carbon, oxygen, and hydrogen, and it differs from alcohol only in having more oxygen in it. It is made, therefore, by adding the requisite quantity of oxygen to the alcohol. Ether, another quite common substance obtained from alcohol, differs from it only in having less oxygen and hydrogen, the carbon being the same in both.

Questions.—About what kind of substances am I to tell you in this chapter? What is said about cider and wine? What kind of change is produced by fermentation? What substance in the fermenting liquids is changed? What kind of a substance is formed from it? In what is the sugar changed? Give the comparisons mentioned. What two things are produced in the change, and how? How can you show that the sugar does not change of itself? In what way does yeast change it? Give the comparison about sulphuric acid. How is the change produced without yeast in making cider and wine? What takes place in the fermentation of bread? Explain the effervescence of bottled cider, Champagne, etc., when the cork is drawn? Why is it that the gas collects in these liquids? In making alcoholic drinks from barley, rye, etc., what change must first be produced? Explain the making of malt. How is the alcoholic liquid made from this? What is said of making whisky? How is the making of vinegar somewhat like the making of alcohol? What is done to the alcohol to change it to acetic acid? What other changes is this like? How is the oxygen added to the alcohol in cider? How much of the cider is changed? How much acetic acid is there in vinegar? What effects the change in the vinegar fermentation? Describe and explain the quick mode of making vinegar. How is the air made to circulate very freely among the shavings? How is the heat causing this produced? What is said of the substances noticed in this chapter? How do acetic acid and ether differ from alcohol?

CHAPTER XXXII.

VEGETATION.

Every plant comes from a seed. When the seed is put into the ground, a root shoots downward into the earth, and a stalk shoots upward into the air.

Observe how the root and the stalk are made. They are not made as the crystals are. Particles are not laid on layer after layer, as in the growth of a crystal. There is no life in a crystal, but there is in the seed. It is this life that forms the plant, and it has its own way of doing it. As it builds the stalk and root, it makes channels or tubes as it works along; but there are no such tubes in a crystal.

Through these tubes the sap goes every where in the plant. This is true of every plant, from the smallest to the largest. Look at some very large and high tree. The life in a little seed made that. It pushed up the stalk a little higher and higher, making tubes in it all the while; and now that it reaches up so high, the sap goes up from the very ends of the roots, in these tubes, out to the very ends of its myriads of leaves.

Let us see now of what the seed from which all this comes is composed. It is mostly starch and gluten. But both of these substances are insoluble. Of what use, then, can they be in growth, if they can not be carried up in the sap that circulates in the plant? Unless they can be rendered soluble they can be of no use. They must remain just there in the seed. But just exactly this change is produced in them. As the seed becomes moist, some oxygen is absorbed, and by this means the gluten is made soluble, and the starch is changed into sugar, which you know is soluble. So as fast as the channels are made in the up-shooting plant, the sap, with gluten and sugar dissolved in it, mounts up in them.

You see now the explanation of the formation of sugar in the sprouting seeds of barley in preparing it for the making of beer, as described on page 207.

But all this is merely to set the plant a going. When the little root is formed, and the stalk reaches the air and puts out leaves, the seed is all done with. Its gluten and starch are used up, and the plant now gathers all its materials for growth from the soil and the air. It must have carbon, oxygen, hydrogen, and some nitrogen. As you have before learned, it obtains from the air a large part of its carbon, taking it in at every pore in its leaves. Its oxygen and hydrogen it gets mostly from the water that comes into the mouths of the roots.

From whence comes the nitrogen that it wants? It may want considerable, for it may be a plant that has gluten in its fruit or seeds. At any rate, it wants some for its leaves.

There is a plenty of nitrogen all about plants, for four fifths of the air is nitrogen. But, though their leaves are bathed in it all the time, though it is at the very door, as we may say, of every little pore, yet not a particle of it enters. All the nitrogen which the plant gets comes up from the ground. There are various substances there that supply it. One is ammonia, which, you learned *on page* 97, is composed of nitrogen and hydrogen. There is a

... of this substance in some manures, as you can know by ... The stronger is the ammonia smell in guano, the bet-...

... have seen that carbon, oxygen, hydrogen, and nitrogen ... grand ingredients in vegetables or plants. You have ... also that the three first of these compose the frame-work, ... There is no nitrogen in woody fibre in any of its ... but this is found only in some of the fruits and juices. It ... there as a part of the food of animals. Plants gather up ... from the earth, and deposit it within themselves for the ... man and other animals. It is deposited just where it is ... For example, there is none of it lodged in the stalk of ... but it is deposited in the seed or grain, so that we can have ... flour with which we make our bread.

... are some other things in vegetables besides those which ... mentioned, but in much smaller amount. I have already ... of silica or flint as being in the stalks of grain and spires ... (page 151). In many vegetables, as mustard and the ... there is considerable sulphur. Then there are phosphorus, ... potash, iron, etc. All these are carried up in the sap through ... channels of which I told you in the first part of this chapter.

... think what sap is. Most of it is water, and this has dis-... in it all the various substances which I have mentioned as ... in plants. Water, then, not only furnishes the plant with ... and hydrogen, but it is the means by which the other ... needed by the plant are carried about in its channels ... to the very ends of the leaves. Some of the water re-... the plant, giving its oxygen and hydrogen to it to help

form wood, starch, gluten, sugar, etc. But the largest part of it is breathed out into the air through the little pores in the leaves.

The quantity of water that passes up through the channels of plants from the roots is much greater than most people suppose. We can get some idea of this by seeing a little how much passes off from the leaves. Some experiments have been tried in regard to this. It was found that in one case a single cabbage breathed out from its leaves into the air, in the course of twenty-four hours, nearly a quart of water. If so much comes from a cabbage, how much must all the leaves of a huge tree throw out into the air from all its leaves.

In all juicy fruits there is much water. In the watermelon there is so much that it gives the name to the fruit. This is almost all water, with a little sugar dissolved in it. The cells that contain this juice are really wood, but very delicate, even more than those of the orange (page 189), and having a great deal of water mingled with it.

It is the water in leaves and flowers that give them their softness. You know how stiff the leaves of flowers are when pressed and dried by the botanist in his herbarium; it is because the water is all gone from their cells.

You know how readily the stalks of grass and of grain bend before the wind, and then rise up again, giving the wavy motion which is so beautiful in a field of grain. This is because there is so much water in the cells and channels of the stalks; but when the stalks of grain are dry, as you see in straw, they will not bend much.

When wood is just cut it is said to be green; that is, it is full [illegible]. As sap is mostly water, there is much water in the wood. [illegible] prevents its burning well; but if it be left to lie in the air, [illegible] passes off into the air, and so the wood becomes dry. [illegible] wood is burned there are ashes. These make but little [illegible] compared with the wood. There is a pound or two of ashes [illegible] a hundred pounds of wood. What has become of the re[illegible], the ninety-eight pounds of the wood? It has flown off [illegible] the air. As a large part of the wood comes from the air, so [illegible] of it, in burning, returns to the air. Much of what passes [illegible] water, for even what we call dry wood contains considera[illegible] water. It passes off in vapor. Then most of the carbon of [illegible] wood, uniting with oxygen, flies off as carbonic acid. Some [illegible] the oxygen of the wood is disposed of in this way, and some of [illegible] unites with the hydrogen of the wood to form water, which [illegible] off as vapor. If this were all, the smoke would not be visi[illegible] for you can not see either vapor or carbonic acid gas; but [illegible] of the carbon goes up in little particles, and these make the [illegible] a thing that you can see.

What is really the composition of ashes? They are composed [illegible] potash, silica, lime, iron-rust, etc. These substances are found [illegible] different proportions in the ashes of different plants. Thus [illegible] is more of silica in the ashes of straw than in those of com[illegible] wood. There is much potash in the ashes of wood, and for [illegible] reason they are used for obtaining that substance for use in [illegible] soap, as noticed on page 131.

Let us look a little more at what plants get from the ground to [illegible] them grow, and how they do it. They get all of the dif[illegible] ingredients, except carbon, from this source. Most of this they get from the air, but some of it comes from the ground. They get, then, from the ground all their oxygen, hydrogen, and nitrogen, and part of their carbon, and, besides these, small quantities of the various things which they need in addition, as potash, lime, iron, sulphur, phosphorus, etc.

Now much of all these ingredients comes from the decay of plants. Every year great quantities of dead leaves and other parts of plants become a part of the earth, and help to form the plants of another year. You can make barren sand good rich earth by mingling with it decayed or decaying vegetable substances. If, in a garden, you have a pit into which you throw all the weeds and small trimmings from trees, you can dig out from it, in two years of time, the richest kind of earth, the result of the decay. I have mentioned this because you are not too young to learn something about gardening.

It is thus that decay and death furnish material for new life. The living beauty that feasts our eyes in the spring comes, to a great extent, from what fell to the ground and died the previous year; and not only so, but that which in its putrefaction offends our sense of smell, becomes a part of the plants which, with their leaves and flowers, so delight our eyes, and the fruits which are so pleasant to our taste. The nitrogen, which is one of the ingredients of the ammonia that you smell so strongly in the manure of the stable, goes up the channels of the wheat-stalk, and helps to make the gluten of the grain, and as you eat it in the bread it helps to form the substance of your body.

You see that there are few ingredients in plants, chiefly four, carbon, oxygen, hydrogen, and nitrogen; but out of these, with [illegible] these a little of some others, are formed a vast variety of [illegible]. I will notice a few of them.

There are some substances that are composed of only two of [illegible] ingredients of plants, carbon and hydrogen. To this [illegible] belong the oils of orange-peel, lemon, and pepper. The oil [illegible] turpentine is also one, and that very singular substance so [illegible] used now for a great variety of purposes, caoutchouc, or [illegible]-rubber.

Then there are some oils that are composed of three of the four [illegible] ingredients of plants, viz., carbon, oxygen, and hydrogen. [illegible] these are the oils of peppermint, valerian, anise, orange-[illegible], rose-petals, etc. Camphor, also, is composed of these three [illegible]dients.

There are some oils that have considerable sulphur in them, as [illegible] of mustard, onion, assafetida, etc. You know that a spoon, if [illegible] in mustard, becomes dark-colored. This is because the sul[illegible] in the mustard unites with the silver to form a sulphuret of [illegible].

There are various acids in vegetables. These are composed of [illegible], oxygen, and hydrogen, in different proportions. I have [illegible]ticed some of these in the chapter on acids, as the tartaric, the [illegible] acid of grapes, and the malic, the acid of apples, pears, [illegible] some other fruits. The only difference in composition be[illegible] these two acids is that the tartaric acid has a little more [illegible]xygen than the malic acid.

There are many different coloring substances in vegetables, as [illegible]digo, the coloring matter of logwood, etc. They are composed, [illegible] the acids, of carbon, oxygen, and hydrogen, or of these with [illegible]trogen.

There is an interesting class of substances brought to light of late years by chemists which I will just notice. There is quinine obtained from Peruvian bark, morphine from opium, theine from tea and coffee, nicotine from tobacco, etc. Nicotine is one of the most deadly poisons in the world. It takes less than a drop of it to kill a rabbit, if put upon his tongue.

Questions.—What takes place when a seed is put into the ground? How are the root and stalk made differently from crystals? What is said about the sap in plants? What is said about a large tree? Of what substances is a seed composed? What change is needed in these, and how is it effected? What becomes of the seed? After the seed is gone, from what is the plant nourished? What materials of growth must it have? How does it get its carbon? How its oxygen and hydrogen? What is said about its needing nitrogen? What about its not getting it from the air? How does it get it? What is said about guano? Of what elements are the substances in plants made? Where in plants is nitrogen deposited, and for what purpose? Mention some other substances that are in some plants? What is sap? What is said of the uses of the water in sap? What of the quantity of water that passes through plants? What of juicy fruits? What of water in leaves and flowers? In the stalks of grass and grain? In wood? How much of wood that is burned becomes ashes? What becomes of the rest? Give the particulars. Why is smoke visible? What substances are in ashes? What do plants get from the ground? What is said of decay as furnishing materials for growth? What can you do profitably with weeds in a garden? What is said of putrefying substances? What of the ammonia in manure? What is said of the formation of all the variety of substances in plants? Which two of the grand ingredients of plants form some of these substances? Mention some substances composed of these? What oils are composed of three of the grand vegetable elements? What is the composition of camphor? What oils have considerable sulphur in them? What is said of vegetable acids? What of coloring substances? From what is quinine obtained? From what morphine? From what theine? From what nicotine? What is said of nicotine?

CHAPTER XXXIII.

CHEMISTRY OF ANIMALS.

[illegible] blood is to an animal what the sap is to a vegetable. The [illegible] water, having dissolved in it whatever is necessary to the [illegible] or building up of the plant; and so the blood is water, [illegible] dissolved in it whatever is necessary to the growth or [illegible] up of the animal.

[illegible] four fifths of the blood in us is water; that is, in every [illegible] pounds of blood there are four of water. You will, of course, [illegible] to know what substances are dissolved in this; that is, what [illegible] up the other fifth of the blood. They are carbon, oxygen, [illegible], nitrogen, chlorine, sodium, potassium, magnesium, iron, [illegible], and sulphur.

[illegible] substances, you see, are elements, not compounds. But [illegible] do not appear as elements in the blood. They are united [illegible] in various ways. For example, the iron is united with [illegible] of the oxygen, forming oxyd of iron, and some of this oxyd [illegible] with phosphoric acid, making phosphate of iron. So [illegible] of the chlorine is united with the metal sodium, forming [illegible] salt, giving to the blood a saltish taste. Then we have [illegible] phorus, oxygen, and calcium united together to form phos- [illegible] of lime, of which, you learned on page 148, there is so much [illegible] bones. About one third of that part of the blood which is [illegible] water is albumen. This is the same substance as white of [illegible] the albumen which you learned on page 200 is found in many vegetables. This is composed of the four grand elements, carbon, oxygen, hydrogen, and nitrogen.

How do all these different substances get into the blood? They come from the food that we eat. All that part of the food which will serve to nourish the body is drank up by little mouths in the stomach, and is put into the blood and becomes a part of it. It is exactly as the little mouths in the roots of a plant suck up from the earth what is proper to go into the sap. The fact that the root of a plant and the stomach of an animal thus perform similar duties is fully illustrated in Chapter IV. of the Second Part of the Child's Book of Nature.

But all the substances that are in our blood are not always in our food. How is it, then, that the blood is always supplied with them? It is because the food contains what these substances are made from. There is some chemistry done in the stomach. It is a sort of chemical laboratory. Great chemical changes are produced there in what is put into it. For instance, you eat, in one way and another, considerable sugar; but there is no sugar in the blood. How is this? Is all this sugar lost? No; it is all used, but it does not go into the blood as sugar; it helps to make some other things that go into the blood.

There is salt in our blood, and there is salt in our food. Here we have a substance that is not altered by the chemistry of the stomach, as sugar is, but goes into the blood as salt.

There is one substance, all of which does not get into the blood from the food; a part of it goes in by the lungs as we breathe. This is oxygen, the lung-food that I told you about on page 16.

All the different parts of the body, as I told you in Chapters I.

and II. of the Second Part of the Child's Book of Nature, are made out of the blood. For this purpose the blood, containing all these different substances that I have mentioned, goes or circulates around every where in the body; and just what materials are wanted for building are used just where they are wanted. For example, where it is necessary to make bone, the materials for bone are taken from the blood, and are arranged so as to make the bone of the right shape. Phosphate of lime is one of these materials, as I told you on page 219. This is in the blood, all ready for use.

So, where there is nerve to be made, those materials are taken from the blood of which nerve is composed; and the same is true of all other parts of the body. Once in a while there is a mistake in this matter. For instance, bony substance is formed in some part where it is not wanted, as in the arteries or in the heart. But, generally, every thing is put in the right place.

Brain and nerve are composed of a variety of substances—a white fatty substance, a red fatty substance, albumen, phosphorus, sulphur, potash, lime, magnesia, etc. Phosphorus is an essential ingredient in brain; that is, the brain can not do without it. I have heard it recommended as a good thing for persons that study to eat freely of eggs, because they contain considerable phosphorus. I do not believe, however, that this would make a bright scholar out of a dull one. Something else besides egg-eating is needed for that.

In hair, feathers, bone, and nails there are sulphur and silica, or flint, mingled with the other ingredients.

There is iron in the blood. It is in the substance that gives the red color to this fluid. Very little of it is to be found ever in any of the solid parts of the body. There is none in the nerves, though it is common to speak of persons who have much firmness of character as having iron nerves. There is a very little of it in the hair, helping, with the silica or flint, to give it strength. Exactly of what use it is in the blood we do not know. When persons are pale and weak they have not enough of it in the blood, and we give them medicines that have iron in them.

You have seen what a variety of substances there is in the blood. Now when one eats a variety of food, it is easy to see how all these various substances are furnished to the blood. But how is it with a child that lives only upon milk? Can there be mingled together in that white fluid all the substances that I have mentioned? If they were not there would be something missing in the building up of the body. If, for example, there were no phosphate of lime in milk, the infant living on milk would have its bones grow, but they would be soft, and would bend very easily, for it is the phosphate of lime that makes them hard and stiff. Milk contains this, and all the other substances that are required for the growth of the body. It contains all the nutritious substances which you can gather from meats and vegetables united together.

There are exactly the same elements or ingredients in milk that there are in blood; but they are not all put together in the same way, and so the milk is different from the blood. Milk is made from blood, and blood is made from milk, and they are really only two different forms of the same thing. The milk of the cow is *made from her blood* by a chemistry which we do not understand,

and when we take it into our stomachs the chemistry there changes it back again into blood. How the iron is kept in the milk, and is prevented from coloring it red, as it does the blood, we do not know.

No matter how many different articles we eat, the nutritious part of them all, which is taken and put into the blood, is a whitish fluid very much like milk; it is called chyle. This fluid is separated or extracted from all the meat, and potato, and rice, and squash, and turnip, and cabbage, etc., etc.; and it contains all that is needed to form bones, teeth, brain, skin, nerves, muscles, nails, hair, etc., with one single exception—I mean the oxygen which it gets from the air in the lungs. The chyle goes to the lungs in the blood to get its supply of oxygen; and now it becomes a part of the blood, and is ready to go to any part of the body to nourish it.

Questions.—Give the comparison between sap and blood. How much of the blood is water? What elements are in the blood? Mention some of the combinations of these in the blood. What is said of the albumen in the blood? How does the blood get all the substances that are in it? Give the comparison between the stomach of the animal and the root of the plant. How is it that there are some substances in the blood that are not in the food? What is said of the sugar that we eat? What of salt? What is said about lung-food? What is said of the circulation of the materials for building different parts of the body? What of making bone? What of making nerve? What are the substances in brain and nerves? What is said of eating eggs? In what animal structures are there flint and sulphur? What is said of iron in the blood? What is said of the expression iron nerves? What is said of milk? How is milk like blood? How does it differ from it? What is said of chyle?

CHAPTER XXXIV.

CONCLUDING OBSERVATIONS.

It may be well, in this concluding chapter, to look back a little upon the ground that we have gone over.

The whole world is built up chiefly out of a few elements. I have told you, in Chapter XV., that there are a little over sixty elements, and of these about fifty are metals. Most of these exist in small quantities. A few of them are very abundant, as iron, calcium, sodium, aluminum, copper, lead, etc. But the most abundant substances in the world are not metals. They are oxygen, carbon, nitrogen, hydrogen, silicon, sulphur, chlorine, etc. Nearly, if not quite one half of the world is a gas, oxygen. And the four grand elements used in the making up of the earth are oxygen, carbon, hydrogen, and nitrogen. Three of these, you see, are gases. Water, that liquid which is every where, and in almost every thing, is composed of two of them. All living substances, vegetable and animal, are essentially composed either of three of them or the whole four.

One thing is true of oxygen which is not true of any other element, viz., that it forms combinations with all the other elements. With most it unites very readily, with some eagerly; but there are some, as gold, silver, etc., with which it will not unite unless it be forced to do it, as you learned in Chapter XXVII., and when it is united with them a very little suffices to make it part company and fly off.

...us look at a few of the combinations which oxygen forms. ...forms with hydrogen the most abundant of all compounds, ...ter. Mixed with nitrogen and carbonic acid gas, it forms the ...abundant of all mixtures, the atmosphere. It forms, with ...metals oxyds, a very numerous class of substances. It forms ... with nitrogen, sulphur, phosphorus, chlorine, silicon, etc. ... singular acid, silica, is one of the most plentiful hard sub...ces in the earth, being in the granite and many other rocks, ...constituting, for the most part, all the sand of the land and ...and a large portion even of the fertile earth. Then we have ... in all the potash and lime, and in their carbonates; the ...bonates of lime in the forms of limestone, and chalk, and mar...being very abundant substances, sometimes forming even ...ntains. Besides all this, oxygen is one of the chief ingredi... in all living substances.

...t you see the importance of this element not only in its ...ndance, but also in its active agencies. It is no laggard in ...chemical movements which are every where going on; it is a ...ly, busy agent. It is the grand supporter of combustion. It ...s every fire and light burning, and the quick explosions of ...powder and many other substances are produced by it. It ...ntains the life of all animals by entering the lungs continual...ly, and it conveys away carbon from their bodies to the leaves of ...nts by uniting with it to form carbonic acid. It rusts the met...als wherever it can get hold of them, and it has such an affinity ...some of them that they can never be found except in the em...braces of oxygen.

...The changes in the forms of matter from solid to gaseous ...

liquid, and the reverse—changes in which oxygen commonly is so busy—are very wonderful when we look into them. Thus, in the burning of wood, the oxygen of the air unites with the carbon and hydrogen of the solid wood, forming the gas carbonic acid and water, which flies off with the gas in vapor. In one hundred pounds of wood, as I have told you on page 215, we have commonly but about two pounds of ashes. The ninety-eight pounds, which are water and carbonic acid, have flown off into the air. What becomes of them? Let us follow and see. The water gathers in the clouds to fall to the earth, or settles upon the ground in the form of dew. In whatever way it comes to the earth, it goes to work there again, and works chemically, for some of it finds its way into the roots of plants, and helps to form their substance by combining with carbon and nitrogen. That part of the ninety-eight pounds which is carbonic acid floats off to be drank up by leaves, in order to furnish carbon, by chemical operations, to the plants and trees. The oxygen that has thus conveyed, as we may say, the carbon to the leaves, returns again to the air, to the lungs of animals; and some of the carbon thus furnished to plants comes back also to animals in the food which they eat, to do again its chemical work in them.

Many other examples of changes of matter back and forth from one form to another might be given, but this will suffice.

When a solid becomes a gas, or a gas a solid, the change is a very great one. When a solid becomes a gas it occupies a vastly larger space, and the particles must therefore be much farther apart. When this change of bulk takes place suddenly a great effect is produced. It is this sudden change of bulk that gives this force to the explosion of gunpowder. On the other hand, when a gas becomes a solid there is a great condensation, or, in other words, the particles of the substance are brought much nearer together. For example, when oxygen unites with iron, and thus becomes a part of a solid substance, about twenty gallons of the gas are pressed, as we may say, into the small space occupied by a pound of the rust (page 98). The same enormous change in bulk takes place when the carbon in the carbonic acid of the air, taken in by the leaves of a tree, becomes so condensed as to form a part of the solid wood.

In some of the changes which are going on in matter there is a very fine division of the particles. As you see charcoal burning, solid carbon is passing off into the air united with oxygen. The particles of the carbon you see in the solid charcoal, but when they pass off you do not see them. Why? Because they are so finely divided. The division is so fine that not even the microscope can show them to you. So, also, if you examine the sap of grass, that feels very rough from the silica or flint that is on its surface, you can not find any particles of silica in it; but they are there, for it is in the sap that the flint goes up from the ground to get to its place on the surface of the grass. The sap is smooth and limpid, for the flint in it is exceedingly fine, and its particles are wide apart; but, deposited in the coating of the grass, the flint is rough, and scratches your finger, for the particles are there closely united together. So, too, the little iron that is in your blood is very finely divided, its particles being diffused evenly throughout that fluid as it circulates in your arteries and veins.

I have often, in the course of this book, spoken of the difference between compounds and their ingredients. Thus oxygen, the gas that makes things burn, unites with another gas that itself burns, to form a substance which quenches burning. Water is unlike its components in other respects also. It is quite a heavy fluid, while one of its components, oxygen, is nearly as light as air, and the other, hydrogen, is the lightest substance known. So, also, that powerful liquid, nitric acid, is totally unlike the oxygen and nitrogen gases that compose it. Take another example of a different character. Phosphorus is a very inflammable substance, and lime is a biting caustic; but phosphoric acid, composed of phosphorus and oxygen, when united with lime, forms phosphate of lime, the mineral matter in our bones. One of the most striking examples we have in common salt, which is composed of a gas that would kill you by suffocation if you should breathe it clear, and a metal that water will set on fire.

I have occasionally noticed in this book the fact that a substance may appear in different forms, perhaps wholly unlike each other. Thus carbonate of lime appears in the forms of chalk, common limestone, and the pure crystallized marble. Gypsum, or plaster of Paris, presents several forms, some of which are very beautiful. Carbon is one of our most wonderful examples, for nothing can be more unlike than charcoal, blacklead, and the diamond. There is no substance, perhaps, that appears in so large a number of different forms as wood, as you learned in Chapter XXVIII. All this variation in form must be owing wholly to variation in the arrangement of the particles, as the proportions of the ingredients are not varied.

In this variation, the differences in character are much increased if the proportions of the ingredients are varied. You know how different calomel and corrosive sublimate are, yet they are made of the same elements, chlorine and mercury, but in different proportions. The five compounds of oxygen and nitrogen are very different from each other, the contrast between the exhilarating gas and the nitric acid being as great as could possibly be conceived. But the most wonderful examples are furnished to us by the chemistry of life. Wood, starch, gum, sugar, oils, perfumes, coloring matters, poisons, etc., how unlike, and yet they are all made of three elements, a solid and two gases. The same may be said of the variety of compound substances in animals, which are all composed of the four grand elements. It is thus that the Creator shows, in the chemistry of life, the greatest power in producing a vast variety of substances from a very few materials.

The frame-work, as we may call it, of chemistry is quite simple. Most of it may be thus marked out:

Oxygen forms with the metals *oxyds*.
Oxygen forms with carbon, sulphur, nitrogen, phosphorus, chlorine, etc., *acids*.
} These, uniting together, form *salts*.

Sulphur forms with the metals *sulphurets*.

Chlorine, iodine, etc., form with the metals *chlorides*, *iodides*, etc.

Then, in the chemistry of life:

Some vegetable substances are made of *oxygen*, *carbon*, and *hydrogen*.

Other vegetable substances,
And all animal substances,
} are made of *oxygen*, *carbon*, *hydrogen*, and *nitrogen*.

There are some substances that are not included in this plan. This is the case with one of the most important and abundant

s would be

hat this hardly seems

of the character of a

by itself having no re-

substances. It is not

in

with a vast varie-

matter in the world

animals and veg-

all the while

is carried

and they

go. For

carries it

lungs the

of the agen-

dissolves the

Chapter XXII.),

construct their

the grasses and

these and many

substances.

direction: and they

carrying on the

are not only con-

changes in other

substances by bringing them together so that they can act upon each other.

The world, as you have seen by what I have told you in this book, is emphatically a world of change; and in the changes that take place there is no loss, no destruction. When things burn up, as we express it, there is no destruction of any substance, but there is merely change from one form to another, and what seems to vanish in air soon reappears in the solid forms that are growing up all around us. So, when decay takes place, there is no loss of a single particle of matter, but there are only chemical changes bringing about new combinations and arrangements of the particles of the decaying substance. Chemistry is at work every where, not destroying, but pulling to pieces only to rebuild again, and it does the latter quite as readily and rapidly as it does the former.

Questions.—How many elements are there? How many of them are metals? Name some of the most abundant of them. What are the most abundant of all the elements? What are the four chief elements? Which of them is the most abundant? What is said of it? Give what is said of some of its combinations. What is said of its activity as an agent? State in full what is said of the changes that take place in the combustion of wood and in consequence of it. What is said of the expansion and the condensation of matter in chemical changes? Give the illustrations of the fine division of matter in chemical changes. What is said of the different forms in which the same substance may appear? How is it when the ingredients are the same, but the proportions are varied? Give the illustrations. Give the frame-work of chemistry as stated. What is said of water? Give in full what is said of the circulation of matter. What is said of the changes that chemistry is effecting in the world?

THE END.

LaVergne, TN USA
22 March 2011
221172LV00003B/104/P

9 781145 951372